Food Is Love

Food Is Love

Plant-Based Indian-Inspired Recipes
to Feel Joy and Connection

Palak Patel

HARVEST

An Imprint of WILLIAM MORROW

Vaghareli Khichdi

For Vaghar   For Khichdi:
Oil   1 cup Rice
Cloves   1 cup moong Dal
Cumin seed   1 cup Onion chopped
Garlic   1 Potato in cubes
Curry leaves   1 Tomato sliced
Peanuts & Cashews   ½ cup green peas
    asofoetida   1 Carrot
   red green chillies   turmeric
                              salt
                              sugar
                              Dry Red chillies

Add Oil to Pressure cooker and heat.
Put in spices for Vaghar in the order listed
let cook - 1-2 minutes, then add all
ingredients for Khichdi and mix with
Vaghar. Add 4 cups Water add turmeric
until its yellow add salt and a bit of
sugar. Taste water to check salt before
closing Cooker. Cook until 1 whistle blows
and reduce to low heat. Close the Cooker.

Recipe by mummy

For the resilient women in my family:
my grandmothers, my superhero mom,
and my loving sister.

For my dad, thank you for your
unconditional love and support.

To my brothers for being a consistent
source of inspiration and laughter.

You're invited to
join me on a
journey through
my most profound
food memories.

Contents

Introduction

Food & Emotion

Have you ever experienced tears of joy after eating a meal? Or received a kiss from a chocolate dessert that left you breathless? Have you ever bitten into something so decadent it caused an explosion in your mouth? Or tasted something so familiar that it brought you right back to childhood? I have, and these are my most cherished food memories, colored with a rainbow of emotions.

My entire life has been a collection of beautiful experiences fueled by food: the delight of the first bite of a mango, the excitement of picking fruit from a tree, the soothing sound of dal simmering on the stove, the surprise and delight of discovering a new flavor, and the triumph of learning a new cooking technique. My relationship with food is a gift that has helped me form a deep connection to myself and others, one that continuously nurtures. The recipes in this cookbook are inspired by my memories, a symphony of emotions, and stories that I've acquired throughout my life.

The Girl & the Chef

Growing up in India, I was raised in a vegetarian household. I spent the first twelve years of my life living with fourteen of my closest relatives under the same roof. Cooking every meal from scratch for fifteen people was a way of life for us, and I knew nothing else. Having no refrigerator might have contributed to our constant cooking, but it still felt like every meal was a well-thought-out, choreographed production. Food was the center of my world. As a kid, I was always up for an adventure and had boundless curiosity in the kitchen. Being the fiercely independent firstborn child, I defied my mom—who never let me roam freely to eat street food—and snuck out a lot to indulge my novice taste buds. I just couldn't bear to wait until she had the time to take me! At the age of seven, instead of playing with dolls or watching TV, I preferred playing chef at home by making chai and creating my own concoction of stir-fried bread with sprinkled spices for our guests. I relished hearing their yummy sounds of praise. Then there's the feeling of winning the food lottery every time my mom and I went to the neighbors' house to loot their guava tree. Just picture *Willy Wonka and the Chocolate Factory* with guava instead of chocolate. My love of foraging grew from our summer road trips, when my dad would pull over so we could gather tart amla (Indian gooseberries) in my mom's shawl—I can still picture the large amla stains we left on the cream fabric. And then there's the transcendental childhood experience of eating mangoes at peak season in India. These memories have molded my relationship to food and still define me as a chef today.

Coming to America

In 1990, when I was twelve, my family moved to Atlanta, Georgia. I was now the Indian kid growing up in the Deep South of America. Our move came with lots of excitement and plenty of new culture to absorb. For starters, I traded my roti and sabzi (vegetable) lunches for pizza and tacos. I also got smart on how to barter for Tater Tots and French fries at school. My adolescent food palate was expanding.

After school, my three siblings and I would huddle in front of the TV, all scrambling for the remote control. While my sister begged to watch

Tom and Jerry, I just had to watch *The Frugal Gourmet*, hosted by Jeff Smith, who explored the culinary traditions of foreign cultures and countries in each episode. Who would have predicted that while on the hunt for *Sesame Street* I would instead become enthralled by Julia Child and Jacques Pépin?

A society, to a great degree, is defined by its culinary contributions, and a large part of my transition into American culture was through food. Food has been a key ingredient in my life—bridging my two worlds together and enabling me to experience a new culture. My culinary quest went to the next level when I started hosting college dorm-room dinner parties on the weekends. After graduating, I approached my parents about going to culinary school, which was met with lots of resistance. Being the oldest daughter of immigrant parents, I had to set an example for my three younger siblings. My parents wanted me to get a stable corporate job after college. And the one thing I knew was that you never disappoint your Indian parents. So, for the next ten years after graduating, I worked at several multinational companies in Atlanta, San Francisco, and New York.

My time living in San Francisco was without a doubt a culinary highlight of my life. The Ferry Building farmers' markets, eating my first meal at Chez Panisse in Berkeley, and wine-country excursions were just some of the reasons I set my sights on culinary school again. I started collecting innumerable cookbooks and became enamored of the Food Network.

On my thirty-first birthday, I moved from San Francisco to New York and enrolled in culinary school to begin career 2.0, training as a chef at the French Culinary Institute. Everything in life felt right when I put on my spotless white chef's coat and hat for the first day of classes. After graduation, I packed my knives and moved to France to immerse myself in learning French cooking. To my surprise, during that experience I still gravitated to cooking dishes from my childhood. My vegetarian upbringing also played a huge role in my cooking. It's what I know best and what makes me the happiest.

Life came full circle when I got back to New York. I had the privilege of appearing on the Food Network and won two famed competition shows: *Chopped* and *Beat Bobby Flay*. Beating an Iron Chef at the top of his game as a five-foot-tall Indian woman gets you noticed. That media exposure allowed me to continue telling my story and sharing Indian food with millions of people. My grandmothers would have been proud to see me make samosas as a competitor on *Food Network Star*. From these wins and exposure, I secured my first restaurant concept in New York, which was slated to open in the fall of 2020.

My World Changes

The pandemic changed my plans in unexpected and jarring ways, and I made the decision to forfeit my restaurant project and return to Atlanta to be closer to my family. But I was still eager to find ways to stay engaged in the kitchen and continue nurturing my relationship with food despite everything going on in the world. There were moments of bliss—watching people learning to cook for the first time, forming new relationships with sourdough starters, mastering the nuances of making pizza dough, or just getting lost in making favorite recipes repeatedly. As the year progressed, though, the combination of overly cautious trips to grocery stores, endless meal prepping, cleanup, and Zoom fatigue began to zap the joy out of cooking. I needed to get back to that relationship I used to have with food, one that was therapeutic and relaxing. I was seeking a reset. And I had a life-changing one deep in the jungles of Mexico at my first spiritual retreat. The experience left an indelible mark on my life and a lasting positive impression on my heart and mind, which continues to influence my love for life and food. From that deep work, this cookbook was born.

This Cookbook

Food has taught me a new way to communicate. Food and cooking are how I express myself; that is why I am a chef—to express my love for my culture, family, and friends. You could say food is my love language. There's a saying in our culture that food made by loving hands and infused with love just tastes better. I pour so much of myself and so much love into my cooking—it's part of my relationship to food and myself: a harmonious dance of emotions. I decide what I'm making based on the emotion it evokes in me.

You may have chosen this book because you love Indian food, you're trying to eat more plant-based food, or you're familiar with my work; in any case, I'm grateful. I understand that Indian food can seem intimidating, but I'm going to show you that it's not. For starters, nearly a billion families make their own versions of countless Indian recipes every single day—my wish is to include you in that tradition. A fun secret among my mom's friends is that many of them didn't know how to cook when they first got married and had families—they figured it out as they went. They found a way to make their own versions of Indian recipes over time. There's something magical that happens when trying and learning leads to new recipes becoming a regular part of your cooking rotation. Just like I learned from my mom and now make my own versions, my wish is that you will make these recipes your own. My motto is "I'm in love with trying; it gets me to new places."

This cookbook is my way to help you express yourself through food and offer you a chance to discover your own relationship with it. Think of it as an opportunity to create memories with food and be more intentional, present, and open while cooking. You might even establish a new relationship with food by cultivating small meditative moments along the way, engaging your five senses to help make cooking more enjoyable and connected. I wholeheartedly hope you will savor your journey.

To support you on your way, there's a lot of Indian mom wisdom in this book (from my mom and from other moms I've cooked with), because let's face it, moms are the best cooks. Of course, there are a few fundamentals, tips, and substitutes that will give you the confidence to cook Indian food and even inspire you to create your own versions of these recipes. When these recipes become your family favorites, I will have succeeded in my endeavor.

I'm from West India, from the state of Gujarat, and I have the most common Gujarati last name, Patel. My family's farms in India date back four or five generations, so it's no surprise that I wrote this cookbook in their honor. My recipes are tried and trusted, inked with wild combinations discovered through my travels and, most importantly, grounded in my love for plant-based food.

How to cook from this book: I've organized

my recipes according to the mood and emotion I most deeply associate with the dishes and the stories behind them. Vegetable porridge, my mom's vaghareli khichdi, is what I make to show someone I really care about them. Or the joy of seeing blistering air bubbles on my homemade garlic naan. To make preparing these recipes more easily accessible to the home cook, I include information on the adaptable ways to use ingredients, where to source the ingredients, and what substitutions can be made. I know you will find something in these pages to make your heart sing.

With gratitude and love,
Palak

My Indian Pantry

If you're just venturing into Indian cooking, my recommended pantry items can be your starter guide. India, of course, is vast, consisting of many regions, and depending on the region, the cuisine and ingredients change. Growing up, I was fortunate that my mom was curious—and ambitious!—about making foods from different regions. While it's simply not possible to do culinary justice to the country in one cookbook, there are certain ingredients that play a prominent role across regions, and these are the ingredients I find most versatile, for both traditional recipes and those I'm riffing on. Fortunately, getting these essentials is easy and convenient thanks to specialty stores and loads of online retailers—even grocery chains have upped their game when it comes to new ingredients.

A word about "traditional recipes": while it is always admirable to learn the nuances of a dish by making it the traditional way, I feel recipes can also be used simply as frameworks that encourage you to experiment and create your own food memories and that help you find your own joy and rhythm along the way. Our family of fifteen has countless adaptations for our favorite dishes, and this is how I hope you'll approach the recipes in this book. My goal here is to help open the door to new ingredients and spark curiosity to adopt them into your own cooking repertoire. I want you to feel confident when cooking. Adjust the ingredients to create something new, but, most importantly, enjoy the process. The act of cooking becomes better when it's personalized.

About Spice

How did I learn spices as a kid? First, I learned the three Cs of spices that are foundational in good Indian cooking (according to my mom): cumin, coriander, and cayenne. These powerhouse spices were almost always in her recipes. In the section below is a list of the essential spices that I use in everyday cooking, not only in savory dishes but also often in desserts and drinks, followed by simple spice blends that wake up your palate (and provide a great way to repurpose spices hanging around in your cupboard). If you're feeling adventurous, make your own seasoning blend with spices you love or modify a recipe from this book.

Store-bought ground spices are convenient but have a shorter shelf life and can lose their potency faster than whole spices. If you do purchase ground spices, do so from a small-batched, single-sourced spice company or any major Indian grocer. If you're trying out new spices you're not sure you'll love, opt for buying them at bulk shops where you can get small quantities rather than committing to a whole jar.

Moisture, heat, and light are detrimental to

spices, so store them in a dark, relatively cool, and dry place (not above or next to your stove). Most spices have a "best by" date on the container. If they don't, write the date of purchase on the cap; toss out dried herbs and ground spices after a year and whole spices after two years.

My Spice Pantry

Asafoetida (hing): This tiny but mighty spice, dating back some 5,000 years, is essential in Indian cooking. "Asa" means "gum" in Persian, and "foetida" means "stinky" in Latin. Hing is typically paired with lentils to help the body digest and absorb the nutrients. The pungent powder is white or pale yellow and is commonly mixed with wheat flour. Be sure to check the label and buy pure asafoetida or one that's mixed with rice flour for a gluten-free option.

Bay leaves: Bay leaves are the leaves of the bay laurel tree and have a strong savory, slightly sweet flavor and a slightly bitter aftertaste. Whole fresh or dried bay leaves are used to temper oil, can be added to curries, and add flavor to rice.

Cardamom: There are two kinds of cardamom: black and green. Cardamom is a spice that does double duty for sweet and savory cooking in my kitchen. Green, the more common, is used for everything from spice mixes to desserts, snacks, and cocktails. The aroma is light and sweet, with a mild eucalyptus smell. Whole green cardamom (including the pod) is ground when making spice mixes like garam masala. However, when using the seeds in sweets or desserts, gently smash open the pod to remove the small black seeds, discard the outer shell, and lightly crush the fragrant black seeds before using. Black cardamom is stronger,

as it's dried over an open fire and has a smoky flavor. Black cardamom pods are mostly used whole to infuse oils and liquids or ground into a masala mix.

Cayenne: Cayenne is a bold, hot ground red pepper spice that's used in Indian, Cajun, and Creole cooking and hot sauces. The heat is deliciously fierce with a subtle after-kick and best used in moderation. Cayenne can be used in place of Kashmiri chili, but the color is more muted and it packs more heat. Too much cayenne can take your mouth on a fiery journey that will have you wanting a cold yogurt or milk.

Chaat masala: Chaat masala powder is a tangy and savory blend that is typically used to flavor chaat, a type of savory Indian street food. I use it on fresh fruits, vegetables, and other dishes. Chaat masala is usually made with amchur (mango powder), cumin, coriander, dried ginger, salt, black pepper, asafoetida, and chili powder. Some recipes also include black salt, pomegranate seeds, and mint leaves.

Cloves: Dried, unopened flower buds shaped like small nail heads, cloves are dark brown in color and have a strong sweet and spicy flavor. They can be used whole or ground and in both savory and sweet dishes.

Coriander seeds and powder: When crushed or ground, seeds from the cilantro plant (or, as Indians call it, the coriander plant) have a delicate flavor that is both refreshing and lively, with a hint of lemon that adds a burst of brightness to any dish. When used in conjunction with other spices, coriander can create a complex and harmonious flavor profile. The seeds can be used for tadka (infused oil), sautéed for a crunchy topping, crushed, or ground.

Cumin seeds and powder: Cumin is a spice that you will find throughout this book. It's one that I reach for often because it has a distinct warm and earthy flavor, like a warm hug on a chilly day. Whole cumin seeds perfume oil, can be sautéed into a crunchy topping, or can be ground into a power-packed powder. Jarred cumin powder needs to be heated for 30 seconds while cooking before liquid goes in.

Fennel seeds (saunf): Fennel seeds, from the bulbous, frondy fennel plant, look like cumin seeds but are pale green. They contribute a very mild licorice-like taste and scent to curries, stews, bread, desserts, and beverages and are essential for adding sweet and cooling notes to curries and vinaigrettes. The seeds are dried whole and are also sold in a powdered form.

Fenugreek leaves (kasoori methi): The small oval-shaped leaves from the methi plant are edible and cooked like spinach in India. The dried leaves sold as kasoori methi are readily available at most Indian stores, and I consider this ingredient a must. The leaves have a smoky, burnt sugar and syrup smell that pairs perfectly with creamy/buttery dishes like makhani sauce. The dried leaves can be used whole or crushed in cooking or scattered on top as a garnish. There are lots of simple ways to use kasoori methi: sprinkled on roasting vegetables and popcorn or on grilled fruit with olive oil.

Fenugreek seeds (methi): Small caramel-colored fenugreek seeds come from methi, an edible green harvested for both its leaves and seeds, and have a distinctive butterscotch flavor and subtle bitterness. Ground fenugreek is found in spice blends such as garam masala, tandoori masala, and pickling spices, and in dosa batter; the whole seeds are

tempered for vegetables and dal tadka. Dry roasting the seeds enhances their flavor, but they can also be soaked, boiled, or sprouted.

Garam masala: A spice blend that can have up to a dozen different spices, including cumin, coriander, cinnamon, cardamom, black peppercorns, and cloves that are toasted and ground together. The name translates to "warm spices." You can make your own using the recipe in this book (see page xxiii) or opt for store-bought. Garam masala is an all-purpose spice that can be used on roasted vegetables or as a finishing spice in Indian dishes. A little goes a long way.

Kashmiri chili: Grown in the state of Kashmir and recognized for their rich red color, these chilies have fruity notes and a milder heat than cayenne peppers. This is why they're a staple spice in my cooking, especially as an everyday chili powder. Kashmiri chilies, in whole and powdered form, are used in tandoori masala blends. The fresh peppers are long, slender, and bright red, balanced in heat and flavor. It's my preferred chili powder for cooking.

Mango powder (amchur or amchoor): Amchur is a fruit spice, made by drying unripened mango in the sun and then grinding it into a powder. The powder is tangy and citrusy and can replace lemon or lime in recipes for a more complex flavor profile. Used in samosas, chutneys, burgers, and soups, and sprinkled on fruit—it works great as a marinade or can impart a tiny bit of tang to salad dressings.

Mustard seeds: Whole mustard seeds are found in three colors, black, brown, and yellow; you can also buy pre-ground yellow mustard powder. For whole seeds, be sure to buy the tiny mustard seeds rather than the larger ones, as they are more pronounced and sharper in flavor. When heated, mustard seeds release a bitterness that can be somewhat hot and spicy with a slightly sweet aftertaste. The effect is like horseradish or wasabi, with a noticeable kick of heat. Black mustard seeds are the dominant spice in mango and carrot pickles.

Nutmeg: Nutmeg has a warm, slightly sweet flavor and a strong, sharp taste. Indian cooking uses nutmeg more for savory dishes than for sweet. Grate fresh nutmeg into dishes or use ground.

Omani limes: An Omani lime—also known as dried lime, black lime, noomi basra, limoo amani, and loomi—is a lime that has been dried in the sun or in a dehydrator. The limes are typically harvested when they are still green and immature; then they are dried until they are hard and black.

Saffron: Saffron threads are carefully pulled from the crocus flower and have an unmistakable light burgundy color. The delicate floral threads infuse a golden color and warm perfume of roses to dishes. Saffron is used in both sweet and savory recipes. Its distinctive color and aroma are the hallmark of fragrant rice dishes like biryani and desserts like ice cream and kulfi. Saffron is used in small quantities, and is typically bloomed in warm water or milk first. The best way to identify fresh saffron is to look for a deep color—the deeper the color, the better the quality.

Star anise: Star anise is a dried star-shaped fruit that has a sweet licorice-like flavor, like fennel. It can be used whole or ground to perfume rice, stews, and tea.

Turmeric: Turmeric is indispensable in my kitchen. This 4,500-year-old spice from India boasts countless health benefits; it is hailed for its anti-inflammatory effects and packed with antioxidants. The root is dried and ground into a golden powder but is also available fresh at many supermarkets. A little goes a long way. Always take care of your white countertops and clothing, as the spice, whether fresh or ground, can stain.

Make Your Own or Buy a Spice Blend?

If you're buying whole spices, then making your own spice blends is a no-brainer. It lets you control the freshness, customization, and quality; it's cost-effective; and it gives you a chance for discovery.

If you're making blends using ground spices, heat them in a dry skillet for a few minutes on low heat until fragrant. Stir continuously to prevent burning. This process will enhance the flavors of the spices.

If you're not making blends at home, don't worry: I'm also an advocate of the convenience, taste, and ease of premade boxed and jarred blends.

Most families I know here in the United States use premade spice blends, including my mom. There's no better or more convenient way to achieve consistency in taste when it comes to cooking Indian food, so absolutely use them. Boxed spice blends are easy add-ins for roasted vegetables, soups, and stews in everyday cooking.

How to Toast Spices

The one thing that can fundamentally change your cooking? Toasting whole spices! Whole spices and seeds are essentially just sleeping in the bottle. When they are heated, they're given a jolt (like your

How to Grind Your Own Spices

Use a spice grinder or a mortar and pestle.

A dedicated spice grinder is key for unlocking the potential of spices. Electric grinders are inexpensive, convenient, and compact—a real workhorse for cooking with spices. Whether grinding small or large batches of spices, the grinder will do its job quickly.

A mortar and pestle (ideally made of granite) allows for quickly crushing spices, herbs, and more—it's decorative and functional. It's worth the effort when grinding small amounts of spice: you can easily control how fine or coarse the grind, and there's just something romantic about it.

How to Temper Spices (Tadka)

At first glance—or perhaps even after trying it—tempering (tadka) can look intimidating. However, this dynamite technique—heating whole spices in oil—is the backbone of Indian cooking and can transform even the most neutral foods into glorious standout dishes. The key to mastering tadka is to gather all your ingredients in front of you before heating the oil. Like wok cooking, tadka is all about timing—because the spices can burn within seconds. A trick I learned for heating the oil is to toss in a single small seed to check the oil's temperature. If the seed dances at a nice rhythm and sputters evenly, the oil is ready. If the seed sputters quickly and turns dark brown to black, the oil is too hot. If the seed sinks to the bottom, the oil is not hot enough.

first cup of coffee does for you in the morning) that wakes up their aroma and helps release essential oils. If you're skipping this step because of time constraints, try this hack: microwave the spices for 20 to 30 seconds; they should become aromatic. Let them cool, and then grind.

Common Spice Blend Recipes

PAV BHAJI MASALA

MAKES ⅔ CUP

½ cup coriander seeds
2 tablespoons cumin seeds
10 green cardamom pods
2 black cardamom pods
2 star anise
1 bay leaf
One 1½-inch cinnamon stick
1 tablespoon fennel seeds
1 teaspoon black peppercorns
2 teaspoons whole cloves
2 tablespoons Kashmiri chili powder
1 tablespoon amchur (mango powder)
1 teaspoon ground turmeric
1 teaspoon black salt (kala namak)
1 teaspoon ground ginger
¼ teaspoon asafoetida (hing)
¼ teaspoon ground nutmeg

1. Heat a dry 10-inch skillet over medium-low heat and toast the coriander seeds, cumin seeds, green and black cardamom pods, star anise, bay leaf, cinnamon stick, fennel seeds, black peppercorns, and cloves for about 10 minutes, stirring occasionally, until fragrant. Be careful not to burn them. Remove the skillet from the heat and let the spices cool for a few minutes.

2. Transfer the toasted spices to a spice grinder, a mortar with pestle, or a small blender. Grind them into a fine powder. Add the Kashmiri chili powder, amchur, turmeric, black salt, ginger, asafoetida, and nutmeg to the spice mixture and stir to combine.

3. Allow the pav bhaji masala to cool completely before storing in an airtight container in a cool, dry place for up to 3 months.

GARAM MASALA

MAKES 1 CUP

1 cup coriander seeds
¼ cup cumin seeds
20 green cardamom pods
4 black cardamom pods
2 tablespoons black peppercorns
2 teaspoons whole cloves
2 teaspoons fennel seeds
Two 1½-inch cinnamon sticks
3 bay leaves
3 star anise
½ teaspoon ground nutmeg

1. Heat a dry 10-inch skillet over medium-low heat and toast the coriander seeds, cumin seeds, green and black cardamom pods, black peppercorns, cloves, fennel seeds, cinnamon sticks, bay leaves, and star anise for about 10 minutes, stirring occasionally, until fragrant. Be careful not to burn them. Remove the skillet from the heat and let the spices cool for a few minutes.

2. Working in batches, transfer the toasted spices to a spice grinder, a mortar with pestle, or a small blender. Grind them into a fine powder. Add the nutmeg to the spice mixture and stir to combine.

3. Allow the garam masala to cool completely before storing in an airtight container in a cool, dry place for up to 3 months.

NOTE: *Garam masala is best when freshly ground, as it retains its aroma and flavor. However, you can also use pre-ground spices if you don't have whole spices available. Garam masala can vary in its ingredients and ratios based on regional preferences and personal taste.*

BIRYANI MASALA

MAKES 1 CUP

½ cup coriander seeds
3 tablespoons cumin seeds
15 green cardamom pods
3 black cardamom pods
2 bay leaves
Three 1½-inch cinnamon sticks
2 tablespoons fennel seeds
1 tablespoon black peppercorns
2 teaspoons whole cloves
1 teaspoon ground nutmeg
1 tablespoon Kashmiri chili powder
2 teaspoons ground turmeric

1. Heat a dry 10-inch skillet over medium-low heat and toast the coriander seeds, cumin seeds, green and black cardamom pods, bay leaves, cinnamon sticks, fennel seeds, black peppercorns, and cloves for about 10 minutes, stirring occasionally, until fragrant. Be careful not to burn them. Remove the skillet from the heat and let the spices cool for a few minutes.

2. Transfer the toasted spices to a spice grinder, a mortar with pestle, or a small blender. Grind the mixture into a fine powder. Add the nutmeg, Kashmiri chili powder, and turmeric.

3. Allow the biryani masala to cool completely before storing in an airtight container in a cool, dry place for up to 3 months.

TANDOORI MASALA

MAKES ½ CUP

15 green cardamom pods
3 black cardamom pods
3 star anise
One 1-inch cinnamon stick
¼ cup coriander seeds
¼ cup cumin seeds
½ tablespoon black peppercorns
1 teaspoon whole cloves
1 teaspoon fenugreek seeds (methi)
2 tablespoons Kashmiri chili powder (or, for less heat, 1 tablespoon Kashmiri chili powder plus 1 tablespoon paprika)
1 tablespoon amchur (mango powder)
2 teaspoons ground ginger
¼ teaspoon ground nutmeg
⅛ teaspoon asafoetida (hing)

1. Heat a dry 10-inch skillet over medium-low heat and toast the green and black cardamom pods, the star anise, cinnamon stick, coriander seeds, cumin seeds, black peppercorns, cloves, and fenugreek seeds for about 10 minutes, stirring occasionally, until fragrant. Be careful not to burn them. Remove the skillet from the heat and let the spices cool for a few minutes.

2. Transfer the toasted spices to a spice grinder, a mortar with pestle, or a small blender. Grind the mixture into a fine powder. Add the Kashmiri chili powder, amchur, ginger, nutmeg, and asafoetida.

3. Allow the tandoori masala to cool completely before storing in an airtight container in a cool, dry place for up to 3 months.

Dry Pantry

Basmati rice: Buy aged basmati grown in Southeast Asia from a specialty Indian store or online retailer. There's no other rice like it in the world. The grains are long and slender, with a light beige color and an aroma that is distinct. Unfortunately, varieties grown locally are not the same. Making the effort to find quality basmati rice is worthwhile. Always rinse basmati rice before cooking for individually separated grains.

Rose water: A rose-flavored water made by steeping rose petals. The petals are distilled by steam or cold pressed to extract their natural oils. Rose water has a delicate floral scent and a slightly sweet taste.

Sesame seeds: White sesame seeds give a novel crunchy bite to lots of Gujarati dishes. Black sesame seeds are unhulled and have a stronger flavor than white.

Sooji/rava: Granulated wheat, also known as semolina, is sold in coarse and fine versions. I use it for sweet and savory recipes. When it's toasted, it becomes very nutty and aromatic.

Refrigerator or Freezer

Curry leaves: You can coat curry leaves with oil and freeze them in an airtight container for up to 3 months. You can dry the leaves in a 200°F oven for an hour, or until they are completely dried, and store in an airtight container. You can also grind the dry leaves into a powered spice and store in a glass jar for up to 3 months.

Ginger: An entire knob of unpeeled ginger, rinsed and dried, can be frozen in an airtight container

for up to 3 months. Just grate what you need and refreeze. Grating frozen ginger will produce dry, fluffy shreds, and the flavorful juices are left inside the ginger as opposed to all over your tools.

Green chilies: Recipes call for either Thai or serrano chilies for heat. Both can be used interchangeably. Remove the seeds and white membrane to reduce the level of heat. Freeze whole chilies and grate or chop them when needed.

Tamarind: A sour fruit pod that is concentrated and jarred, tamarind is widely used in Indian cooking. The ripe fruit has a dark brown color with a sweet-tart taste. Sold as a paste or concentrate (both available at Asian supermarkets and used interchangeably), it can be added directly to recipes.

Oils

Below are the three kinds of oils I use. All can be used for searing and sautéing.

Coconut oil: Virgin coconut oil is intensely coconut-forward and ideal for baking. Refined coconut oil is milder. You can also use refined coconut oil in recipes that call for a neutral oil.

Neutral oils, such as safflower, sunflower, peanut, and grapeseed oil: The high smoke point and neutral taste are my preference for cooking most Indian dishes. These oils are all great for high-heat cooking like searing, sautéing, grilling, and frying.

Olive oil: Although expensive, extra virgin olive oil tastes great, with its flavor-forward herbaceous, peppery notes and citrusy smell. If you like it and enjoy cooking with it, feel free to use it for these recipes. Refined olive oil is lighter in color and has a higher smoke point than extra virgin olive oil.

Salts

Finishing salt: A gourmet sea salt is a nice luxury to add to finished dishes; you can also put out a small container of it at the table for guests. The snowflake-shaped crystals add a pop of saltiness and texture to salads and grilled foods. I use the Maldon brand.

Indian black salt (kala namak): Kala namak is also known as Himalayan black salt. It's a kiln-fired rock salt that is sulfury and pungent and has a purple or pink hue. A common salt used in India, especially in chaat dishes—it makes street food addictively good because it provides both salty and tart flavors all at once. The sulfuric quality adds an eggy taste to vegan tofu scramble (the alternative for scrambled eggs) or chickpea frittata.

Kosher salt: Kosher salt is slightly coarse and my choice for an everyday salt; I use Diamond brand.

But keep in mind that salt crystal sizes vary by brand, so once you find a brand you like, stick to it. This will make your cooking and seasoning more consistent.

Pink Himalayan salt: A fine-grain salt that dissolves quickly, pink Himalayan is hand-extracted and minimally processed to yield an unrefined product that's free of additives.

Sugars

Certified organic brown sugar (light or dark): Extracted from sugarcane, the dark brown variety contains more molasses than the light brown one.

Certified organic cane sugar: I recommend buying organic cane sugars that are made exclusively from sugarcane. Varieties of cane sugar are sold in unrefined, raw, and refined forms. Certified organic sugars are vegan. Often, granulated sugar, sometimes called table sugar or white sugar, is not vegan because it has been refined using bone char—animal-derived charcoal—to remove impurities during processing.

Pure maple syrup: A staple for baking and cooking, maple syrup is my substitute when I don't want to use sugar. Maple syrup comes from boiling the sap from sugar maple trees. Its flavor is well rounded, with mild sweetness and subtle notes of smoke and even earth.

Practically Plant-Based

If you're new to plant-based cooking, these ingredients will make swapping out eggs and dairy easier.

Aquafaba: This is the liquid from cooked or canned chickpeas that you can save for later use by freezing. Before whipping, pour the liquid into a measuring cup and then heat it in a saucepan to reduce it by one-third in volume. Pour the liquid back in the measuring cup and let it cool. This will make the liquid thicker and viscous so that it whips like egg whites. To stabilize the mixture, add about ¼ teaspoon cream of tartar when whipping. Freeze any extra reduced liquid for later use.

Cashews: Cashews are a natural thickener commonly used in plant-based cooking. Soak them in hot water for 30 minutes or overnight and then puree them in a blender or food processor. The silken cream that results is a fabulous substitute for the dairy in cream-based dishes.

Flaxseed and chia seeds: When ground and combined with water, flaxseed and chia seeds can be used as an egg replacement. It's best to grind small batches of whole flaxseed when you need a flax "egg" in a recipe. Ground flaxseed can also be used as a binder in recipes. 1 egg = 1 tablespoon ground flaxseed or chia seeds + 3 tablespoons water.

Extra-firm tofu and silken tofu: Seared extra-firm tofu is a substitute for paneer (an Indian cheese). Purchase firm tofu that's vacuum-sealed because it has less liquid. Silken tofu is versatile for sweet and savory dishes, like khadi or chocolate pudding.

Frozen Vegetables

I lean on fresh vegetables, but sometimes fresh vegetables are not available or in season. In New York's winter months, the grocery store freezer section is a necessary stop. Frozen produce is picked at peak freshness and flash frozen to retain as many nutrients as possible—that's good news here. Frozen vegetables are also convenient because the prep work is done for you.

Essential Kitchen Tools

When it comes to kitchen gadgets, I think about versatility. Having multiple uses for a piece of equipment justifies the space and investment. Here are some invaluable tools in my kitchen.

A Lodge preseasoned 10.5-inch round cast-iron griddle: This is one of my most used pans for all types of recipes—rotis, dosas, and grilled cheese—and for charring or simply searing vegetables. This pan reminds me of an Indian tava—it's virtually indestructible and easy to clean and maintain.

A small food chopper: I have a small chopper that is phenomenal for chopping onions and mushrooms, pureeing tomatoes, and processing batches of ginger and garlic to freeze in ice cube trays. This speeds up chopping when you're busy.

A good nonstick 8-inch skillet: Essential for pancakes and crepes, a sturdy nonstick pan with a smooth surface uses less oil. Do not use metal tools with it, as they can scratch the surface.

A high-speed blender: Many plant-based recipes call for a high-speed blender, and it's a worthwhile investment. They last forever (I've had mine for more than thirteen years and it's still going). The strong motor blends to a smoother, creamier consistency for soups, batters, nut milks, and nut butters.

An enameled cast-iron 8- or 10-inch skillet: This versatile pan can go from stove to oven. The cast iron on the inside retains high heat and the enameled surface forms a nonstick coating that can handle temperatures far higher than PTFE or ceramic nonstick. Most brands can withstand temperatures of up to 500°F.

A small or midsize wooden rolling pin with handles: Indian rolling pins (velan) are skinnier and have smaller handles for better leverage; these pins are used to roll round rotis and stuffed parathas.

Pulses, aka Lentils

Pulses, edible seeds that grow in a pod, are a part of the legume family and include beans, lentils, and peas. Containing the highest level of protein of any plant-based food, they are essential to the Indian pantry. Dal, as both an ingredient and a dish, is the most common Indian pulse. Growing up, I memorized Indian dals by their color to keep them straight. Here's a quick guide.

Brown/green: Old faithful. These lentils are easily available and used in a variety of dishes, including soups, stews, and salads. They soften a lot when cooked for long periods.

Puy or French lentils (deep moss–colored discs): Posh. French-style lentils are smaller than regular green lentils. The skin is tougher, and the lentil maintains its shape after cooking. Use in salads and soups. Puy is the region in France where these lentils are from.

Masoor dal (red or pinkish lentils): Ambitious. This breakout Indian lentil is readily available at local grocery stores now. A powerhouse dal, masoor cooks quickly and with tinge of sweetness.

Toor dal (split yellow pigeon peas): Main squeeze. Commonly known as arhar dal, this lentil is a silky oval yellow disc that completely melts into a creamy mush when cooked. In traditional dal recipes, this is the go-to lentil.

Green moong: Tough guy. These small green seeds are hard and yellow on the inside, sprouted, and available split with or without skin. Moong beans with their skins look like bright green leafy vegetables. Whole moong can be prepared in a pressure cooker or Instant Pot, but they should be soaked before cooking. Whole moong sprouts are called moong bean sprouts.

Yellow moong (hulled and split yellow beans): Small but mighty. Yellow moong cooks quickly to make basic yellow dal but is also used for desserts and fritters.

Urad dal (white dal): Strong and bold. Urad dal may be a whole black lentil, a whole white lentil without skin, or, the one used in this book, a split dal without skin. The split urad dal is used in dosa batter for a sticky texture and has a bold, tangy smell when fermented.

COOKING TIPS
• *Wash and sift through lentils to remove any debris or pebbles.*
• *Soaking reduces the cooking time and makes the nutrients easier for the body to absorb.*
• *Add a pinch of asafoetida (hing) to lentils to help reduce bloating.*

How to Pinch, Dash & Sprinkle Your Way to Cooking Good Indian Food . . .

As you're cooking with this book, use your palate as a guide and adjust the quantity of any of the spices, garlic, ginger, and salt to your preferred heat level and taste. Ultimately, your version is the best

version. The goal here is to cook with more spices, however you feel comfortable doing so.

Spices ≠ spicy: This is a common misperception. Spices are sweet, cooling, warming, smoky, and tangy; only a few are genuinely hot. Spices have their own unique personality and robustness. In winter months, cooking with spices like cinnamon and cardamom warms up the body, and in summer months, coriander and cumin keep the body cool. You can still enjoy cooking with spices, even if you don't like spicy food.

Salt: The type of salt and its texture does matter. I've found that my own "pinches" of salt are consistent based on the brand I've been cooking with for almost two decades, Diamond kosher. Pink Himalayan salt is my other go-to. Keep in mind the finer the salt, the easier it is to oversalt dishes—believe me, I've done it. If you're unsure if a dish needs salt, put a portion of it into a smaller container and season and taste it before adding it back to the pot.

Salting starches: Don't be shy with salt when seasoning starches like potatoes and lentils because it brings forward the flavors of other spices.

Visual cues: Gravy-based dishes are done cooking when a little of the oil shimmers on top of the dish. This is a sign of a sauce made well.

Curry leaves ≠ curry ≠ kadhi: These may seem similar but they are not the same thing. See the following sections for more on curry.

Stocking up on staples: Whipping up Indian food requires always having on hand onions, garlic, ginger, chilies, and curry leaves (fresh or dried).

Onions: Yellow or Spanish onions are what's used most in Indian cooking. Red onions can be substituted.

Carrots and ginger: No need to peel. Just wash and scrub thoroughly before using.

A Note About Curry

It's best we take a moment to talk about the word "curry," which is technically not an Indian food or a word that describes any Indian dish; it is a British term that was given to dishes that had a sauce or gravy with spices. The term is as generic as "bread" or "pasta," and in India there are many iconic and popularized types of "curries," but they all have very specific names, origins, and rich histories.

Is Curry Powder a Single Spice?

No. Curry powder is misunderstood. It is a mix of many different spices, not a single spice. A true curry will consist of a particular blend of spices to match the ingredients from a specific region, like Madras. While it somewhat resembles the North Indian spice mixture called garam masala with turmeric, there are countless combinations sold as "curry powder." Supermarket curry powder typically consists of coriander, turmeric, cumin, fenugreek, and red pepper, although each brand is different.

Step-by-Step Indian Cooking Basics

1. Heat the fat (oil and/or butter).

2. Temper whole seeds such as cumin, mustard, coriander, fenugreek, fennel, caraway, or coriander (see page xxii). Tempering, also known as tadka, blooming, chonk, or vaghar, is the alchemical process of Indian cooking.

3. Infuse oil with whole spices such as cinnamon sticks, cardamom pods, black peppercorns, cloves, star anise, and bay leaves. These should be removed before eating.

4. Add aromatics—ginger-garlic paste, onions, chilies, fresh curry leaves.

5. Stir in ground spices such as cayenne, turmeric, coriander, cumin, and paprika. Heat these for no more than 30 seconds before adding your next ingredients—ground spices can burn quickly.

6. Pour in liquids such as tomatoes, coconut milk, cream, yogurt, or water.

7. Add your main—vegetables, lentils, and/or protein.

8. Finish with ground spices like garam masala, cream, and fresh herbs.

For step-by-step videos on how to cook some of the recipes in this book, visit:

Food Is
CARING

What food or recipe do you use to show love to others?

Food is one of the most meaningful ways in which we express love and caring for those around us. For me, there's no better way to show someone how much I care than by cooking a delicious meal or baking for them. Whether it's a warm and comforting bowl of dal, a decadent dessert for a birthday, or a multicourse meal. It's deeply satisfying to watch someone enjoy a dish that you've created with your own hands, knowing that you've played a small part in bringing them happiness. For me, cooking and sharing food is not just a practical necessity but also an expression of love and connection.

My most cherished memories are of sharing meals with family and friends, whether it's a cozy dinner at home or a lively gathering with lots of people. Food has a way of breaking down barriers and fostering intimacy and closeness. It's a universal language that transcends cultural and language differences, and it has the power to connect people from all walks of life.

In my experience, the act of cooking itself is also a form of self-care and love. When I take the time to prepare a meal for someone else, I'm not only showing them love and kindness, but I'm also taking care of myself by engaging in a creative and thoughtful activity. There's something meditative and therapeutic about chopping vegetables, stirring a pot, or kneading dough. It allows me to slow down and focus on the present moment, which is a rare and valuable experience in our fast-paced world.

Preparing and sharing food, no matter how simple or elaborate, is an innate act of generosity, kindness, and love that can have a profound impact on the people around us.

Cilantro Chutney   4

Red Garlic Chutney (Lasooni Marchu)   6

Spicy Green Chili Chutney (Thecha)   7

Kale Flatbread (Dhebra)   9

Aromatic Basmati Rice   10

Lemon Rice   12

Yellow Dal (Tadka Dal)   14

Baked Beans & Dried Mint (Tava Beans)   15

Vegetable Barley Soup   18

Braised Beans & Greens   21

Punjabi Kadhi   22

Instant Pot Vegetable Porridge (Vaghareli
   Khichdi)   25

Classic Masala Chai   28

Chai Concentrate   30

Sweetened Iced Chai   31

Cilantro Chutney

MAKES 1 CUP

2 cups tightly packed fresh
  cilantro (about 1 bunch
  leaves and stalks)

½ cup fresh mint leaves

¼ cup raw cashews, peanuts,
  sunflower seeds, or daria
  (see Note)

Juice of ½ lemon (about
  1 tablespoon)

1 Thai chili, or ½ serrano chili

½-inch knob fresh ginger

½ teaspoon ground cumin

2 ice cubes

Kosher salt

It's fitting that an Indian-inspired cookbook starts with the ultimate chutney for cilantro lovers, with mint for a pop of freshness. This chutney is a must-try condiment; it's typically served with fried foods for a zesty kick. The cashews thicken the chutney, giving it a creamy, rich consistency, and they also help it retain its emerald-green vibrancy (see Note). Substitute cashews with peanuts, seeds, or even dried lentils for a similar consistency. A thicker chutney doubles as a dipping sauce and a spread on toast. Adjust the heat level by adding or reducing the chili.

Combine the cilantro, mint, cashews, lemon juice, chili, ginger, and cumin with the ice cubes and ¼ cup cold water in a blender. Blend on high speed until smooth, occasionally scraping down the sides of the blender. Add salt to taste and serve immediately. Store leftover chutney in a glass container for up to 3 days.

NOTE: *A few tips to keep chutney vibrantly green: Add protein like nuts or an Indian dried lentil called daria (also spelled dalia), which thickens the chutney as well, to prevent the cilantro from oxidizing. Add a few ice cubes to cool the blender blades—the heat also oxidizes cilantro.*

Red Garlic Chutney (Lasooni Marchu)

MAKES 1 CUP
1 cup peeled garlic cloves
¼ cup Kashmiri chili powder
1 teaspoon ground cumin
Kosher salt

Lasooni marchu, a garlic chili chutney, is one of the first things my mom taught me how to make. It's a garlicky condiment that comes from the state of Gujarat and is spooned on top of khichdi (porridge). This chutney can be made by hand using a mortar and pestle for a complex flavor, but it also comes together easily in a small food chopper (see page xxvii). The level of heat in this chutney can be reduced by replacing half the Kashmiri chili powder with paprika.

Combine the garlic, Kashmiri chili powder, and cumin in the bowl of a food chopper and pulse three or four times, scraping the sides of the bowl as needed. The chutney should still have some texture. Add salt to taste. Store leftover chutney in an airtight container in the refrigerator for up to 1 month.

Background: Red Garlic Chutney;
foreground: Spicy Green Chili Chutney (opposite)

Spicy Green Chili Chutney (Thecha)

MAKES ½ CUP

1 teaspoon neutral oil

10 Thai chilies

3 green Anaheim chilies

3 garlic cloves

¼ cup salted sunflower seeds

⅓ cup olive oil

Juice of ½ lemon (about 1 tablespoon)

½ teaspoon ground cumin

1 teaspoon coarsely ground coriander seeds

Kosher salt

At the age of seventy-eight, my mom still maintains a garden, and in the summer there's an abundance of chilies. I freeze some and with the remaining ones I make this thecha, a charred green chili chutney that's popular in the state of Maharashtra. The word "thecha" loosely translates to "pounded." The charred peppers are pounded to a coarse-textured paste using a mortar and pestle. The heat level of thecha can vary depending on the type of chili and the amount used, but this chutney is spicy. Thecha is an all-purpose condiment that I add to dishes for an unapologetic punch of heat.

Heat the neutral oil in a medium cast-iron skillet over medium-high heat, then add the Thai and Anaheim chilies and the garlic. Cook, using tongs to rotate every few minutes, until lightly charred on all sides, about 5 minutes. Remove from the heat and transfer the chilies and garlic to a mortar with pestle or a food processor. Add the sunflower seeds and grind to a coarse paste. Transfer to a small bowl and stir in the olive oil, lemon juice, cumin, and coriander. Season with salt to taste and serve. Store leftover chutney in an airtight container in the refrigerator for about 1 week.

NOTES

• Turn on your oven's vent (or hood fan) and crack windows when charring the chilies.

• For a milder chutney, reduce the number of Thai chilies or replace them with serrano chilies.

• A cast-iron skillet works best, or a heavy-bottomed pan will work as well.

Kale Flatbread (Dhebra)

MAKES 12 FLATBREADS

2 cups millet flour

1¼ cups whole wheat flour, plus more for rolling

2 cups finely chopped kale

2 garlic cloves, grated

1-inch knob fresh ginger, grated (about 1 teaspoon)

2 tablespoons white sesame seeds

½ teaspoon ground turmeric

⅛ teaspoon ground cayenne

1 cup plain plant-based yogurt

2 teaspoons kosher salt

¼ cup neutral oil

NOTES

• This dough does not need to rest.

• Use a small food chopper to chop the kale more finely.

• Substitute any hearty green of your choice for the kale.

My champa ba (grandmother) had a chakki, a hand-operated mill made of two heavy stones and a wooden handle to rotate the plates, to grind grains. As a kid, I spent every summer at her house and always pleaded to help with the mill. She told me stories while she worked, and I loved being her helper by scooping up the flour. Millet, or bajari, is the humble grain that is used to make dhebras with fresh fenugreek leaves (kasoori methi). Because methi is not readily available in many grocery stores, in this recipe I replace it with kale. Serve with a side of pickles or your favorite dip.

1. Combine the flours, kale, garlic, ginger, sesame seeds, turmeric, cayenne, yogurt, and salt in a large bowl. Add water, a tablespoon at a time, until the dough comes together and is slightly sticky, 2 to 3 tablespoons. Then knead the dough into a ball. Coat the dough ball with a teaspoon of the oil.

2. Portion the dough into 12 equal pieces and then shape them into round balls by rolling each piece between your palms.

3. Heat a dry 8-inch nonstick skillet over medium heat. Flour a work surface. While the skillet is warming, roll a dough ball in the flour and then roll it out into a 5-inch disc with a rolling pin. If the dough sticks, re-form it into a ball again and start over.

4. Gently place one disc on the skillet, cook for 1 minute, then flip it with a spatula. Brush ½ teaspoon of the oil over the surface of the flatbread and cook until light brown spots appear. Flip it again and brush another ½ teaspoon oil on the top. Continue to cook, flipping two or three times more, gently pressing and moving the flatbread with a spatula until light brown spots appear on both sides. Repeat with the remaining dough balls.

Aromatic Basmati Rice

MAKES 4 CUPS

1 tablespoon plus 1 teaspoon
   neutral oil

1 cup basmati rice

1 bay leaf

One 1½-inch cinnamon stick

1 star anise

1 tablespoon kosher salt

The word "basmati" means "fragrant" in Hindi, and this rice smells nutty and floral. Basmati rice is a long-grain rice that has a distinct aroma and delicate texture; its exquisite taste from aging is unmatched by any other rice variety. Unlike short-grain rice, basmati grains remain separated when cooked. Basmati is ideal for making biryanis and pulaos and as a side for most Indian dishes. This method cooks the basmati rice like pasta, in a rolling boil of water with salt, which eliminates the need for measuring out water.

1. Drizzle 1 tablespoon of the oil across an 18 × 13-inch baking sheet. Set aside.

2. This is the most important step for fluffy basmati rice: Place the rice in a large bowl and add cold water to cover. Gently, to avoid breaking the long grains, run your hand through the water and the rice to remove dust and starch. When the water turns cloudy, drain the rice, return it to the bowl, and refill the bowl with cold water. Repeat the process three or four times until the water runs clear. (Alternatively, you can rinse the rice in a fine-mesh strainer under running water in the sink until the water runs clear.)

3. Return the rice to the bowl and cover with 3 cups cold water. Soak for 30 minutes, then drain the water from the rice.

4. Place the bay leaf, cinnamon stick, and star anise in a large saucepan, add the remaining 1 teaspoon oil, and fill with water. Bring to a boil over high heat, then add the salt. Gently scoop the rice into the water, give it a stir, and let boil for 1 to 2 minutes. Reduce the heat to medium. The rice will float to the top like pasta. Start checking for doneness after about 8 minutes. The rice should be tender but not mushy. If it still has some bite, cook for an additional 2 minutes, then check again. Drain immediately and carefully spread it on the prepared baking sheet to cool; this additional step prevents the rice from

NOTES

• *The rice can be made ahead and cooled. Reheat in a covered glass bowl in the microwave or in the top of a double boiler.*

• *To make cumin rice, replace the bay leaf, cinnamon, and star anise with 1 teaspoon cumin seeds.*

sticking together. Discard the aromatics, if desired, or save them for a garnish. Once the rice has cooled for about 10 minutes and every grain has grown a little longer and is separated, transfer the rice to a serving bowl and serve.

Lemon Rice

SERVES 2 TO 4

1 tablespoon neutral oil

½ teaspoon black
  mustard seeds

⅛ teaspoon asafoetida (hing)

¼ cup raw cashews

1 Thai chili, sliced lengthwise
  (optional)

¼ teaspoon ground turmeric

Juice of 1 lemon (about
  2 tablespoons)

2 cups leftover white rice

Kosher salt

NOTE: *The Thai chili
can be substituted with
a small serrano chili.*

Lemon rice (chitranna) is from South India, and it's a stir-fried-rice dish. The rice is cooked and cooled to room temperature before tempering it with spices and curry leaves. It can be served warm or at room temperature.

Heat the oil in a large skillet or wok over medium heat until it is shimmering. Add the mustard seeds and cook until they sputter, about 1 minute. Stir in the asafoetida and cashews and stir-fry until the cashews are lightly golden, about 1 minute. Mix in the Thai chili (if using), turmeric, and lemon juice. Add the cooked rice to the skillet, season with salt to taste, and stir well to combine. Serve the lemon rice hot or cold, as a side dish or a main meal. Remove the Thai chili after cooking, if desired.

Top right: Lemon Rice (opposite);
bottom left: Yellow Dal (page 14)

Yellow Dal (Tadka Dal)

SERVES 4

1½ cups yellow moong dal, chana dal, masoor dal, or a combination

Kosher salt

½ teaspoon ground turmeric

1 tablespoon neutral oil

½ teaspoon cumin seeds

¼ teaspoon asafoetida (hing)

1 yellow onion, finely chopped

3 garlic cloves, minced

1-inch knob fresh ginger, grated (about 1 teaspoon)

1 medium Roma (plum) tomato, finely chopped

1 Thai chili, chopped

¼ teaspoon ground cayenne

2 teaspoons ground coriander

1 teaspoon ground cumin

Juice of ½ lemon (about 1 tablespoon)

Tadka

3 tablespoons neutral oil

1 teaspoon cumin seeds

1-inch knob fresh ginger, grated (about 1 teaspoon)

1 large garlic clove, thinly sliced

½ teaspoon Kashmiri chili powder

¼ teaspoon asafoetida (hing)

Learning to make dal is an instant way to connect to Indian culture and cuisine. Dals are made plain with just turmeric and salt for when you're under the weather, but they can also be enhanced with tadka (see page xxii). Serve it with lemon rice, plain rice, or naan.

1. Wash the dal in a strainer under running water in the sink until the water runs clear. Place it in a large bowl, cover with water, and soak for 30 minutes. Drain the water and set the dal aside.

2. In an Instant Pot, or in a heavy-bottomed pot, combine the dal, 4 cups water, 1 teaspoon salt, and the turmeric. In the Instant Pot, cook on the pressure cook setting for 5 minutes. In the pot, bring to a boil, reduce the heat, and simmer until the dal is cooked and soft, 20 to 25 minutes. Set aside.

3. Heat the oil in a large skillet over medium heat. Add the cumin seeds and cook until they sputter, about 30 seconds. Stir in the asafoetida.

4. Add the onion to the skillet and sauté until it turns light golden brown, 5 to 7 minutes; stir in the garlic and ginger and cook for about 1 minute, until fragrant. Add the tomato and Thai chili and cook until the tomato softens, about 5 minutes. Add the cayenne, coriander, and ground cumin and cook until fragrant, about 30 seconds. Add the mixture to the cooked dal. Simmer for 15 to 20 minutes, stirring occasionally. Add ¼ cup water if the dal becomes too thick. Taste and adjust the seasoning with additional salt if desired.

5. **Make the tadka:** Heat the neutral oil in a small skillet over medium heat. Add the cumin seeds and cook until they sputter, about 30 seconds. Add the ginger and garlic and cook until the ginger is lightly golden, about 30 seconds. Add the Kashmiri chili powder and asafoetida and stir until fragrant, about 30 seconds. Pour the tadka over the dal, stir well, and serve.

Baked Beans & Dried Mint (Tava Beans)

SERVES 4 AS A SIDE DISH

2 tablespoons neutral oil

1 medium yellow onion, thinly sliced

4 garlic cloves, thinly sliced

Kosher salt

2 tablespoons tomato paste

1 red bell pepper, cored, seeded, and cut into 1-inch pieces

1 tablespoon all-purpose flour

1 tablespoon paprika

1 teaspoon Kashmiri chili powder

Freshly ground black pepper

Two 15-ounce cans cannellini beans, rinsed and drained

1 bay leaf

1 tablespoon Dried Mint (recipe follows on page 17), or ¼ cup fresh mint, chopped

NOTE: Crushed red pepper flakes or hot paprika can be substituted for Kashmiri chili powder in this dish, and store-bought dried mint can be used instead. Substitute butter beans or large white beans for the cannellini beans

I have a love affair with beans and legumes. Years ago, I attended a wedding in Bulgaria, and while in the region, I visited the neighboring country of Macedonia. My friend's mom took me to the local market and taught me how to make their traditional tavče gravče, a slow-cooked baked bean dish with smoked paprika and mint. I consumed copious amounts of rezha, a hot red pepper native to Macedonia that is available fresh or dried. I learned that "tavče" refers to the clay pot that the dish is cooked in; an Indian word for skillet, "tava," is similar. My baked beans recipe uses a blend of paprika and Kashmiri chili powder.

1. Preheat the oven to 350°F.

2. Heat the oil in a large Dutch oven over medium heat until it is shimmering. Stir in the onion, garlic, and 1 teaspoon salt and cook until the onion is translucent, 4 to 5 minutes. Stir in the tomato paste and bell pepper and sauté to soften the bell pepper, about 3 minutes. Sprinkle the flour over the pepper mixture and stir until a thick paste forms, about 2 minutes. Reduce the heat to low and cook, stirring frequently, until the flour is fully incorporated, about 5 minutes. Add the paprika and Kashmiri chili powder, then season with salt and black pepper to taste. Stir until fragrant, about 30 seconds.

3. Stir in the beans and add enough water to cover. Add the bay leaf, cover the pot, and transfer to the oven. Bake until the liquid in the beans is vigorously bubbling on the surface, about 1 hour. Remove from the oven and let cool for 10 minutes. Remove and discard the bay leaf. Taste and adjust the seasoning as needed. Scatter the mint on top and serve hot.

Dried Mint

MAKES ¼ CUP

2 cups tightly packed fresh
  mint leaves, washed and
  dried

Place the mint on a paper towel and microwave for 1 to 2 minutes, checking every 40 seconds, until dried. Crush into a powder using your hands or in a mortar and pestle and store in a small airtight container until ready to use. It will keep for up to 1 month.

Vegetable Barley Soup

SERVES 4 TO 6

2 tablespoons neutral oil

1 medium yellow onion, diced

Kosher salt

1 celery rib, cut into ½-inch pieces

1 medium carrot, cut into ¼-inch dice

6 ounces cremini mushrooms, thinly sliced

3 garlic cloves, minced

½ teaspoon ground fennel

½ teaspoon ground coriander

¼ teaspoon ground turmeric

Freshly ground black pepper

1 quart (4 cups) vegetable broth

2 cups cooked pearl barley, cooled

1 medium zucchini, cut into ¼-inch dice

1 teaspoon lemon juice

⅓ cup Cilantro Chutney (page 4)

Ready to fall in love with spring vegetables all over again? As my first internship out of culinary school, I worked in a small restaurant in the south of France. Early mornings, I would accompany the chef to pick fresh vegetables from a nearby farm. I ran specials at the restaurant, and this version of classic French vegetable pistou (pesto) soup with dolloped chutney on top has been my spring go-to soup since.

1. Heat the oil in a large Dutch oven over medium heat until it is shimmering. Add the onion and 1 teaspoon salt and sauté for about 3 minutes, until lightly translucent. Stir in the celery, carrot, and mushrooms and cook until the vegetables are softened, 8 to 10 minutes. Stir in the garlic and cook until fragrant, about 30 seconds. Stir in the fennel, coriander, turmeric, and a couple of grindings of pepper and cook until fragrant, about 30 seconds. Add the broth and barley and simmer for 15 minutes.

2. Stir in the zucchini and cook until tender but still green, 3 to 5 minutes. Add the lemon juice and season with salt and pepper to taste. Divide the soup among bowls and serve each topped with a generous tablespoon of chutney.

Braised Beans & Greens

SERVES 6

2 pounds hardy greens, such as kale, mustard greens, or collard greens (about 2 bunches)

3 tablespoons neutral oil

1 small yellow onion, cut in half and sliced

1-inch knob fresh ginger, minced (about 1 teaspoon)

Kosher salt

2 garlic cloves, minced

2 teaspoons ground turmeric

1 teaspoon ground coriander

1 teaspoon Garam Masala (page xxiii) or store-bought

Freshly ground black pepper

¼ cup Scrappy Indian Bouillon Cubes (page 138; about 4 frozen cubes)

One 14-ounce can unsweetened coconut milk

One 15-ounce can chickpeas, drained and rinsed

1 Fresno or serrano chili, sliced

This is where Scrappy Indian Bouillon Cubes come in handy. Braising hardy, leafy greens in coconut milk and pairing them with hot chilies and spices gives this side dish a full range of bitter, spicy, and warming tastes. These greens are amped up with chickpeas for added protein.

1. Remove the tough ribs and stems from the bottom half of the greens and reserve for making broth another time. Cut all leaves into 1-inch strips.

2. Heat the oil in a large skillet over medium heat until it is shimmering. Add the onion and ginger and season with 1 teaspoon salt. Cook, stirring often, until the onion is softened, about 5 minutes. Add the garlic, turmeric, coriander, garam masala, and black pepper, stirring to evenly distribute. Cook until fragrant, about 1 minute. Stir in the bouillon cubes until they have dissolved.

3. Add the coconut milk and chickpeas to the skillet and bring to a simmer. Stir in the greens a portion at a time, letting them wilt slightly before adding more. Cook, tossing occasionally, until the greens are tender and the mixture looks creamy, 15 to 18 minutes. Taste and season with more salt and pepper if needed.

4. Transfer to a shallow platter or bowl and top with chili slices.

NOTE: *This dish can also be made with tender greens like spinach or arugula. Reduce the cooking time to 2 to 3 minutes, until the greens are wilted.*

Punjabi Kadhi

SERVES 4

Baked Fritters (Pakoras)

1 cup chickpea flour

1 small Yukon Gold potato, peeled and grated

1 small yellow onion, thinly sliced

½ cup finely chopped kale (optional)

2 garlic cloves, minced

1-inch knob fresh ginger, grated (about 1 teaspoon)

1 Thai chili, chopped

½ teaspoon ground cumin

¼ teaspoon ground coriander

1 teaspoon amchur (mango powder)

1 teaspoon kosher salt

¼ teaspoon baking soda

Kadhi

One 16-ounce package silken tofu, drained

½-inch knob fresh ginger

½ cup chickpea flour

¼ teaspoon ground turmeric

¼ cup fresh lemon juice (from about 2 lemons)

1 Thai chili, chopped

Kosher salt

NOTE: *The kadhi calls for a fair bit of lemon juice to help add sourness to the silken tofu. You can also substitute lime juice for the lemon juice.*

Kadhi is a traditional North Indian dish, a thickened stew with yogurt and chickpea flour. Onion and potato fritters (pakoras) made with chickpea flour and spices are fried and added to the kadhi. To prevent the yogurt in the sauce from curdling, the stew must be constantly stirred during cooking. I tweaked the recipe to make it plant-based by pureeing silken tofu in the blender and discovered that the tofu has the same thick consistency as yogurt without breaking. Mind-blowing, right? My version uses baked fritters instead of fried, although you could fry the pakoras if you prefer.

Tadka

3 tablespoons neutral oil

½ teaspoon cumin seeds

2 black or green cardamom pods

¼ teaspoon fenugreek seeds (methi)

1 teaspoon coarsely ground coriander seeds

⅛ teaspoon ground cloves, or 3 whole cloves

¼ teaspoon asafoetida (hing)

2 to 3 whole dried red chilies (optional)

Kosher salt

1 teaspoon ground fenugreek (methi), for garnish

1. **Make the baked fritters:** Preheat the oven to 350°F. Line a baking sheet with a silicone baking mat or parchment paper.

2. In a large bowl, combine the chickpea flour, potato, onion, kale (if using), garlic, ginger, Thai chili, cumin, coriander, amchur, and salt. Stir in ½ cup water to make a thick batter. It should come together but not be cakey. Add the baking soda and mix well. Use a tablespoon to measure the batter onto the prepared baking sheet. Bake for 20 to 25 minutes, until the fritters are lightly golden outside and cooked in the center.

(recipe continues)

3. Make the kadhi: Place all the ingredients in a high-speed blender, add 4 cups water, and puree until smooth, about 1 minute. Taste and adjust the seasoning as desired.

4. Make the tadka: Heat the oil in a wide heavy-bottomed saucepan over medium-high heat until it is shimmering. Add the cumin seeds and cook for 30 seconds, then add the cardamom pods, fenugreek seeds, coriander seeds, and cloves and cook for another 30 seconds. Add the asafoetida and dried red chilies.

5. Reduce the heat to medium. Slowly pour the khadi mixture into the tadka, then stir to combine. Add the pakoras and simmer for 20 to 25 minutes. Season with salt to taste.

6. Sprinkle the ground fenugreek over the top and serve hot with rice or Layered Bread (Lacha Paratha) (page 169).

Instant Pot Vegetable Porridge (Vaghareli Khichdi)

SERVES 4 TO 6

1 cup short-grain white rice

1 cup lentils, such as split red lentils, split green moong beans, or toor dal

2 tablespoons neutral oil

1 teaspoon cumin seeds

1 medium yellow onion, chopped

1 medium carrot, chopped

1 small Yukon Gold potato, peeled and diced

1 medium Roma (plum) tomato, diced

2 cups chopped cauliflower

2 garlic cloves, minced

1-inch knob fresh ginger, grated (about 1 teaspoon)

One 1½-inch cinnamon stick

1 teaspoon ground turmeric

½ teaspoon ground cayenne

⅛ teaspoon asafoetida (hing)

⅛ teaspoon ground cloves

Kosher salt and freshly ground black pepper

Toppings

Yogurt Sauce (Chaas) (recipe follows on page 27)

Red Garlic Chutney (Lasooni Marchu) (page 6)

Based on an ancient Ayurvedic food, vaghareli khichdi is an endlessly diverse dish of vegetables, rice, and lentils cooked down like a porridge. It's nourishing and recommended for balancing the body, and my mom's khichdi was the only thing I craved when I moved away for college. Vaghareli khichdi starts with a small medley of whole spices as the base, with sautéed vegetables layered on top. My mom's khichdi is how she shows love, and no matter where we travel together as a family, if she has access to a pot, we get khichdi (see Note)—even in Scotland!

1. Place the rice and lentils in a fine-mesh sieve and rinse under cool running water until the water runs clear. Transfer to a large bowl, add fresh water to cover, and soak for 15 minutes.

2. In the meantime, heat the oil in the inner pot of an Instant Pot or other multicooker on the sauté setting until it is shimmering. Add the cumin seeds and cook until the seeds sputter and are fragrant, about 30 seconds. Stir in the onion, carrot, potato, tomato, cauliflower, garlic, ginger, cinnamon stick, turmeric, cayenne, asafoetida, cloves, 1 tablespoon salt, and ¼ teaspoon black pepper. Drain the rice and lentils and add them to the mixture with 3 cups fresh water. Set the Instant Pot to pressure cook on high for 11 minutes. When the cooking time is up, let the pressure release naturally. Taste and adjust the seasoning with additional salt and black pepper if desired. Divide the khichdi among shallow bowls and serve with yogurt sauce and red garlic chutney.

NOTE: *This recipe can be made in a Dutch oven or a heavy-bottomed pot with a lid. Cover and cook over medium-low heat for 45 minutes, or until the rice and lentils are fully cooked and the vegetables are tender.*

Yogurt Sauce (Chaas)

MAKES 2 CUPS

1 cup plain plant-based yogurt

⅓ cup chopped fresh cilantro

¼ teaspoon ground cumin

Kosher salt

Khichdi is served with chaas, a diluted yogurt sauce. It cools the palate and coats the mouth to protect it from hot food. My dad likes drinking chaas as a soup. I prefer it as a topping for khichdi.

Whisk together the yogurt, 1 cup water, the cilantro, and cumin in a small bowl. Season with salt to taste. Serve at room temperature or cold.

Classic Masala Chai

MAKES 4 CUPS

2 cups plain oat milk

2 teaspoons Indian loose-leaf chai or black tea

½ teaspoon Masala (recipe follows)

1 tablespoon cane sugar, or to taste

My mom once told me her first cup of hot tea in the morning is the secret to calming and grounding her for the day, and I agree—I always feel better after a cup of chai. The classic masala chai is made with loose-leaf black tea, steeped with spices and milk. My mom has been making the same chai recipe in the same small steel saucepan for as long as I can remember. Most Indian families have their own trusty saucepan for making chai, and the recipe remains unchanged for decades and is passed down through generations. Her steel saucepan epitomizes nostalgia. So pick a metal saucepan and give this traditional recipe a try—who knows, over time that little saucepan may become your family heirloom.

Combine the oat milk with 2 cups water in a medium saucepan and add the loose tea and masala. Bring to a rolling boil over high heat, then reduce the heat to a simmer. Stir in the sugar and simmer to steep for 5 minutes. Bring to a boil again and then immediately remove from the heat. Strain the tea and enjoy.

Masala

MAKES ¼ CUP

20 green cardamom pods

1 tablespoon fennel seeds

½ teaspoon black peppercorns

¼ teaspoon whole cloves

One 1½-inch cinnamon stick

1 tablespoon ground ginger

¼ teaspoon ground nutmeg

Heat a dry 10-inch skillet over medium-low heat and toast the cardamom, fennel, black peppercorns, cloves, and cinnamon stick for about 10 minutes, stirring occasionally, until aromatic. Cool for a few minutes, then transfer the mixture to a spice grinder and grind to a fine powder. Add the ginger and nutmeg. Store the masala in an airtight container in a dry, cool place for up to 1 month.

Background: Sweetened Iced Chai (page 31);
foreground: Classic Masala Chai (opposite)

Chai Concentrate

MAKES 1 QUART (4 CUPS)

12 green cardamom pods

4 star anise

Three 1½-inch cinnamon
sticks

6 whole cloves

2 tablespoons fennel seeds

2 tablespoons black
peppercorns

¼ cup fresh ginger, roughly
chopped

¼ teaspoon freshly grated or
ground nutmeg

⅓ cup cane sugar

¼ cup loose-leaf black tea

Pinch of baking soda

I completely understand that making classic masala chai from scratch may not be feasible if you're not a tea drinker. Rest easy, you can use this chai concentrate to make hot tea, mocktails, cocktails, and iced chai on the fly. Just make a large batch and refrigerate it.

1. Heat a large heavy-bottomed saucepan over low heat and add the cardamom, star anise, cinnamon sticks, cloves, fennel seeds, and black peppercorns. Toast until aromatic, 5 to 7 minutes. Add 1 quart filtered water, the ginger, nutmeg, and sugar.

2. Bring the mixture to a boil over medium-high heat, then immediately reduce to a low simmer to steep. Allow the mixture to gently simmer for 10 to 12 minutes.

3. Remove from the heat and let cool for 30 seconds. Stir in the tea and baking soda and let steep for 5 minutes.

4. Strain the mixture through a fine-mesh strainer into an airtight glass jar with a tight-fitting lid. Discard the solids. Store the chai in the refrigerator for up to 1 month.

Sweetened Iced Chai

SERVES 2

¼ cup Chai Concentrate
    (opposite)

Ice

2 thinly sliced lemon rounds,
    for garnish

This book wouldn't be complete without a sweet iced tea. This recipe is the marriage of chai from India and the tradition of iced tea from the American South.

Mix the chai concentrate with 1 cup water in a pitcher. Fill two glasses with ice, pour the tea over the ice, and garnish each glass with a lemon round.

Food Is
NOSTALGIC

What smells or foods conjure memories of home and family for you?

When you find yourself yearning to click your heels and be transported back to childhood, it's a smell that can instantly take you there. Our sense of smell is like a time machine, capable of unlocking doors to memories and emotions we believe had long been sealed away.

Food is at the top of the list for evoking nostalgia because it's a mental snapshot of a moment in time. The dishes we savor carry with them the weight of time, each bite a journey through our history. Food is like a tapestry interwoven with threads of how our cultural and social identities were formed—how we created a sense of belonging and connection.

Even today, the smell of okra transports me back to my family's tiny kitchen in India and gives me a sense of joy. I have a mental image etched of my mom's fingers delicately stuffing each slender okra pod, her hands stained with turmeric, reminding me of henna. The smell of cooking okra filled every nook and cranny of our house, so whenever I catch a whiff of okra, memories of my family gathered on the floor to eat with our hands, sharing stories, come to the surface, and I'm reminded of their love and warmth.

Smell is a testament to the enduring power of food, capable of preserving not only memories but also the bonds of love and togetherness that define the concept of home.

Cranberry Chutney

MAKES 2 CUPS

1 pound fresh cranberries

1 tablespoon neutral oil

¼ teaspoon black
  mustard seeds

½ cup light brown sugar

¼ cup apple cider vinegar

1-inch knob fresh ginger,
  grated (about 1 teaspoon)

⅛ teaspoon ground cloves

⅛ teaspoon ground cayenne

Kosher salt

NOTE: *Use frozen
cranberries if fresh
berries are not
available.*

The one thing that's never missing on my Thanksgiving menu is cranberry sauce, and since sauces are like chutneys, I make this recipe year-round. To echo the qualities of chutney, this recipe has bloomed mustard seeds, ginger, and other ground spices added to the cranberries; the brown sugar balances the tartness. The ingredients are simmered together until the pectin-rich cranberries burst open and the mixture develops a deep jewel-like color.

1. Rinse the cranberries, removing and discarding any stems or soft berries.

2. Heat the oil in a medium saucepan over medium heat until it is shimmering. Add the mustard seeds and cook until they sputter, about 1 minute. Stir in the cranberries, brown sugar, vinegar, ginger, cloves, cayenne, and ½ cup water. Cook, stirring occasionally, until the cranberries burst and the mixture thickens, 10 to 15 minutes.

3. Stir in 1 teaspoon salt, then taste and adjust the seasoning as needed. Let the chutney cool to room temperature. Transfer to an airtight container and store in the refrigerator for up to 2 weeks.

Indian Ketchup (Kasundi)

MAKES 1 CUP

1 tablespoon neutral oil

½ teaspoon black
  mustard seeds

One 15-ounce can crushed
  tomatoes

¼ cup white vinegar

½ teaspoon fresh lemon juice

3 tablespoons brown sugar

½ tablespoon Kashmiri chili
  powder

¼ teaspoon ground coriander

¼ teaspoon ground cumin

¼ teaspoon ground turmeric

⅛ teaspoon asafoetida (hing)

Kosher salt

NOTE: *Cane sugar
can be substituted for
brown sugar in this
recipe.*

This is the best amped-up ketchup. A versatile homemade ketchup-style chutney, kasundi can be an accompaniment for rice or naan, a spicy condiment for grilled cheese and burgers, or a dip for fries.

1. Heat the oil in a medium saucepan over medium heat until it is shimmering. Add the mustard seeds and cook until they sputter, about 1 minute. Add the crushed tomatoes, vinegar, lemon juice, brown sugar, Kashmiri chili powder, coriander, cumin, turmeric, and asafoetida and stir to combine. Reduce the heat to low and simmer until the tomatoes break down and the oil starts to separate from the mixture, stirring occasionally, 20 to 25 minutes. Season with salt to taste. Remove the pan from the heat and let the kasundi cool to room temperature.

2. Transfer the kasundi to an airtight container and store in the refrigerator for up to 2 weeks.

Baked Squash & Dal Muffins (Handvo)

MAKES 24 MINI MUFFINS

Neutral oil, for greasing

⅔ cup white rice

⅔ cup toor dal (see Note)

2 cups grated yellow squash

¼ cup plain plant-based yogurt

2 garlic cloves, grated

1-inch knob fresh ginger, grated (about 1 teaspoon)

1 tablespoon cane sugar

½ teaspoon baking powder

½ teaspoon baking soda

¼ teaspoon ground cayenne

¼ teaspoon ground cumin

¼ teaspoon ground turmeric

2 teaspoons kosher salt

Juice of ½ lemon (about 1 tablespoon)

Tadka

2 tablespoons neutral oil

1 teaspoon black mustard seeds

2 teaspoons white sesame seeds

⅛ teaspoon asafoetida (hing)

10 curry leaves (optional)

Cranberry Chutney (page 36) or Cilantro Chutney (page 4), for serving

NOTE: *You may substitute masoor dal for the toor dal.*

Handvo is a fermented rice and dal snack that originated in Gujarat. Trays of baked handvo remind me of southern corn bread. The dish originated to use up leftover rice and dal, which are ground and mixed with vegetables and spices to make a savory batter that's baked. My siblings and I compete for the crust, so my mom started baking them in a muffin tin—this way each serving has its own crust. These are served at breakfast or as an afternoon snack with tea.

1. Preheat the oven to 350°F. Grease a 24-cup mini muffin pan with oil.

2. Rinse the rice and dal in a fine-mesh strainer under cold water until the water runs clear. Transfer to a medium bowl, add water to cover, and soak for 4 hours. Drain the water, transfer the rice and dal to a food processor or blender, and grind to a smooth paste. Scrape the mixture into a large bowl. Add the squash, yogurt, garlic, ginger, sugar, baking powder, baking soda, cayenne, cumin, turmeric, salt, and lemon juice. Mix well to form a batter. Divide the batter into the prepared wells of the muffin tin.

3. **Make the tadka:** Heat the oil in a small saucepan over medium heat until it is shimmering. Add the mustard seeds and cook until they sputter, about 1 minute. Add the sesame seeds and asafoetida, then remove from the heat. Add the curry leaves, if using. Spoon the tempered oil with the optional curry leaves on top of the batter in the muffin tin.

4. Bake for about 25 minutes, until a toothpick inserted in the center of a muffin comes out clean. Serve hot or at room temperature with your choice of chutney.

Tofu Scramble (Bhurji)

SERVES 4

2 tablespoons neutral oil

1 small yellow onion, chopped

Kosher salt

2 medium Roma (plum) tomatoes, diced

1-inch knob fresh ginger, grated (about 1 teaspoon)

1 garlic clove, minced

1 Thai chili, or ½ serrano chili, seeded

½ teaspoon ground turmeric

½ teaspoon Kashmiri chili powder or paprika

½ teaspoon Pav Bhaji Masala (page xxiii) or store-bought

½ teaspoon black salt (kala namak)

One 14-ounce package extra-firm tofu, drained and finely crumbled

1 small green bell pepper, cored, seeded, and diced

Juice of ½ lime (about 1 tablespoon)

Freshly ground black pepper

Indian Ketchup (Kasundi) (page 37), for serving

If you're skeptical about tofu for breakfast, this tofu bhurji recipe can convert you. Bhurji is a style of scrambled eggs in India popularized by street vendors and eaten for breakfast, lunch, or dinner. When I was growing up, my dad owned a poultry farm where he sold eggs. I remember running around barefoot chasing chickens and holding fresh eggs in my hands. My dad made anda (egg) bhurji with vegetables on overcast mornings served with roti or fresh white bread. I've re-created that dish using extra-firm tofu. When it's cooked down with the tomatoes, turmeric, and spices—including a little black salt, the secret ingredient I learned from street vendors—it's close to scrambled eggs.

1. Heat the oil in a large skillet over medium-high heat until it is shimmering. Stir in the onion and 1 teaspoon kosher salt. Sauté until the onion is lightly browned, 7 to 10 minutes, stirring occasionally. Stir in the tomatoes, ginger, garlic, chili, spices, and black salt. Cook until the tomatoes have completely softened, about 5 minutes.

2. Scatter the crumbled tofu over the onion mixture and thoroughly mix. Cook until the tofu is warmed through and well-seasoned, 5 to 7 minutes. Add the bell pepper, lime juice, and black pepper to taste and cook for another 3 minutes. Taste and season with additional salt and black pepper as desired. Serve hot with Indian ketchup.

Steamed Vegetable & Oat Cakes (Idlis)

SERVES 6

1 cup old-fashioned
  rolled oats

½ cup semolina flour

1 tablespoon neutral oil, plus
  more for greasing

½ small yellow onion,
  chopped

½ teaspoon ground cumin

½ teaspoon kosher salt

⅛ teaspoon asafoetida (hing)

½ cup grated carrot (1 small
  carrot)

½ cup grated zucchini
  (1 small zucchini)

¼ cup frozen peas, thawed

½ cup plain plant-based
  yogurt

1 Thai chili, chopped
  (optional)

½-inch knob fresh ginger,
  grated (about ½ teaspoon)

½ teaspoon baking soda

½ teaspoon fresh lemon juice

Cilantro Chutney (page 4),
  for serving

Idlis are a staple of a South Indian breakfast. They are an undisputed classic, made by steaming a batter of fermented rice and urad dal. Freshly made soft, pillowy idlis melt in the mouth and are often on my breakfast menu. I grew up eating savory breakfasts, not sweet. In fact, I crave only savory foods in the morning. When I don't have time to ferment rice, I make this oatmeal version that has all the goodness of idli, instantly.

1. Add 2 inches of water to a stovetop steamer or pasta pot with strainer and bring to a gentle simmer. Lightly grease six 6-ounce ramekins and set aside.

2. Heat a 10-inch skillet over medium-low heat and add the oats and semolina flour. Cook, stirring frequently, until the mixture is light golden brown and smells fragrant and nutty, about 15 minutes. Remove from the heat and transfer it to a medium bowl.

3. Wipe the skillet clean, add the oil, and heat over medium heat until the oil is shimmering. Add the onion, cumin, salt, and asafoetida. Cook, stirring occasionally, until the onion is translucent, 2 to 3 minutes. Transfer to the bowl with the oat mixture.

4. Stir in the carrot, zucchini, peas, yogurt, Thai chili (if using), ginger, baking soda, lemon juice, and ⅓ cup water. Mix well to combine. Using a ¼-cup measure, spoon the mixture into the prepared ramekins. Working in batches, stack the ramekins in the steamer. Cover and steam until the batter has risen and set, about 15 minutes. Remove and cool for a few minutes, then unmold from the ramekins and serve with chutney.

NOTE: *The batter can be made the night before and rehydrated with a few tablespoons of water.*

Charred Chaat Masala Okra

SERVES 2 TO 4

½ pound fresh okra

1 tablespoon neutral oil

1 bunch scallions ends trimmed and cut into thirds

2 teaspoons chaat masala

Kosher salt

½ lemon (about 1 tablespoon juice)

During the photo shoot for this cookbook, I made this okra recipe for the team. It was such a hit! The okra is cooked in the style of smoky shishito peppers—charred with scallions in a cast-iron skillet until crisp and blackened on the outside and tender on the inside. To finish the dish, I sprinkle on some fresh lemon juice, which adds a bright, zesty note that complements the chaat masala.

1. Rinse the okra with cold water and pat dry with a clean kitchen towel.

2. Heat the oil in a large skillet over medium-high heat. Working in batches, add the okra and scallions to the skillet in a single layer. Cook for 3 to 4 minutes, until the vegetables start to blister and char on one side.

3. Flip and cook on the other side for an additional 3 to 4 minutes, until charred and tender. Sprinkle the chaat masala and salt to taste over the okra and toss to coat evenly. Squeeze the lemon juice over the top and serve hot as a snack or side dish.

NOTE: *Turn on the exhaust fan and open windows. For a darker charred exterior, cook for another 3 to 5 minutes.*

Stuffed Okra

SERVES 4

1 pound 4-inch-long okra
(about 36)

¾ cup chickpea flour

1 teaspoon white
sesame seeds

4 garlic cloves, grated

1-inch knob fresh ginger,
grated (about 1 teaspoon)

2 teaspoons ground cumin

½ teaspoon ground cayenne

½ teaspoon amchur (mango
powder), or 1 teaspoon
fresh lemon juice

½ teaspoon cane sugar

Kosher salt

3 tablespoons neutral oil

Recipes are tributes, and this stuffed okra dish certainly is one—to my mom, who taught it to me. It's no surprise that there are recipes that can easily flood us with emotions—nostalgia, joy, and gratitude. They speak volumes about family and tradition through the art of cooking. Preparing this dish is not just about re-creating my mom's recipe; it's about preserving a piece of her and sharing it with love.

1. Rinse the okra with cold water and pat dry with a clean kitchen towel. Using a paring knife, trim the top and bottom off. Carefully make a slit lengthwise in the okra. Do not cut all the way through end to end—you want to create more of a pocket than an open-ended taco.

2. Combine the chickpea flour, sesame seeds, garlic, ginger, cumin, cayenne, amchur, sugar, and ¼ teaspoon salt in a large bowl. Working over the bowl, use your fingers to gently stuff the center of each okra with filling. Reserve any remaining mixture to add to the dish once the okra is tender.

3. Heat the oil in a large skillet with a lid over medium heat until it is shimmering. Add the stuffed okra, filling side up, and reduce the heat to medium-low. Cover and cook until the okra is bright green, about 10 minutes. Remove the lid and sprinkle any reserved filling on top of the okra. Cook, uncovered, until the extra filling is absorbed and the okra is tender, about 10 minutes. Taste and adjust the seasoning, adding more salt if desired, and serve immediately.

Potato Peanut Shaak

3 tablespoons neutral oil

1 teaspoon cumin seeds

⅓ cup shelled raw unsalted peanuts

2 tablespoons white sesame seeds

10 curry leaves

3 pounds Yukon Gold potatoes, peeled and cut into 1-inch cubes

1 Thai chili

1 teaspoon cane sugar

¼ teaspoon ground cayenne

Kosher salt

½ cup chopped fresh cilantro, for garnish

My mom has single-handedly turned potatoes into a dish I dream about. These potatoes are stir-fried with peanuts, curry leaves, and white sesame seeds, then topped with fresh cilantro. They're crunchy, herby, spicy, and simply irresistible. Next time you're in the mood for breakfast hash potatoes, switch things up with this recipe. Trust me, there will be a mad scramble to eat leftovers, if anything is left.

1. Heat the oil in a large skillet with a lid over medium heat until it is shimmering. Add the cumin seeds and cook until they sputter, about 30 seconds. Stir in the peanuts, sesame seeds, and curry leaves and sauté for another minute. The peanuts will become lightly golden and aromatic.

2. Add the potatoes, Thai chili, sugar, cayenne, and salt to taste. Stir to combine, reduce the heat to low, and cook, covered, for about 25 minutes, stirring occasionally, until the potatoes are tender. Remove from the heat and garnish with the cilantro. Serve warm.

Gingery Cabbage Shaak

SERVES 4

2 tablespoons neutral oil

1 teaspoon cumin seeds

⅛ teaspoon asafoetida (hing)

1 medium red onion, thinly sliced

3-inch knob fresh ginger, julienned (see Notes)

Kosher salt

½ teaspoon ground turmeric

¼ teaspoon ground cayenne

2 medium Roma (plum) tomatoes, diced

1 small head green cabbage (about 2 pounds), thinly sliced into long ribbons (see Notes)

2 tablespoons dried fenugreek leaves (kasoori methi)

1 teaspoon lime juice

My dad is not much of a cook, but he did learn this cabbage dish from one of his colleagues and made this for us with dal on cold nights. The sweetness that emerges when the hearty cabbage is cooked with the addition of spicy ginger gives this dish a new dimension. You could also make this with tender cabbages, like napa or savoy, by sautéing until slightly wilted.

1. Heat the oil in a large skillet or wok over medium-high heat until it is shimmering. Add the cumin seeds and cook until they sputter, about 30 seconds. Sprinkle in the asafoetida, then stir in the onion, ginger, 1 teaspoon salt, the turmeric, and cayenne. Cook until the onion is translucent, 5 to 7 minutes.

2. Stir in the tomatoes and cabbage. Cover and cook for about 20 minutes, until the tomatoes have softened and the cabbage is tender. Remove the lid and season with salt to taste. Sprinkle with the fenugreek leaves, drizzle with the lime juice, toss, and serve warm.

NOTES

• You can grate the ginger instead of julienning it, but the long strands provide a nice texture for the dish.

• Using a sharp knife, cut the cabbage head into quarters, remove the core, set each wedge on a flat edge, and cut downward to slice into long ribbons.

Salted Coconut Lassi

SERVES 2

2 cups plain almond or
  coconut yogurt

½ cup unsweetened
  coconut cream

¼ cup pure maple syrup

1 tablespoon rose water

¼ teaspoon kosher salt

Tart, creamy yogurt lassis have many variations, both sweet and salty. A traditional yogurt lassi was a regular thing for me until I adopted a plant-based diet. I experimented with different kinds of alternative yogurts and found that almond and coconut are closest in taste to the traditional drink. This recipe also contains a hint of rosewater fragrance.

Combine the yogurt, coconut cream, maple syrup, rose water, salt, and 1 cup water in a high-speed blender and blend until smooth. Adjust the consistency as desired by adding more water. Pour into glasses and serve cold.

Mango Lassi

SERVES 4

4 cups chopped ripe honey
  mangoes (from about
  3 mangoes), or 4 cups
  frozen (see Note)

2 cups plain plant-based
  yogurt

2 cups barista-style plain
  oat milk

1 tablespoon pure
  maple syrup

1 tablespoon fresh lemon
  juice (from about ½ lemon)

¼ teaspoon ground
  cardamom, for garnish

Mint sprigs, for garnish

I've drunk my fair share of mango lassis in my lifetime. Slurping down lassis with mint is how I'd always enjoyed my beloved summer drink—that is, until I learned another family tradition: adding a little ground cardamom on top. Believe it not, I'd never thought about doing that.

For this recipe, you can use any ripe mango variety that's in season or opt for frozen mangoes if fresh are not available. I like barista-style oat milk, which is thicker and creamier in consistency.

Combine the mango, yogurt, oat milk, maple syrup, and lemon juice in a high-speed blender and puree until smooth. Pour into four glasses and garnish each with a pinch of cardamom and a sprig of mint.

NOTE: *Increase the maple syrup by 1 tablespoon if using frozen mangoes, which are less sweet than fresh.*

Thandai Milkshake

SERVES 4 TO 6

Thandai Masala

¼ cup raw almonds

¼ cup raw cashews

¼ cup raw unsalted pistachios

1 teaspoon fennel seeds

½ teaspoon ground cardamom

½ teaspoon ground cinnamon

¼ teaspoon black peppercorns

¼ teaspoon freshly grated nutmeg, plus more for garnish

One 14-ounce can coconut whipping cream, such as Nature's Charm, chilled

Milkshake

⅛ teaspoon saffron threads

4 cups barista-style plain oat milk

3 tablespoons pure maple syrup

1 pint vegan vanilla ice cream, softened

When I have a hankering for a milkshake, I make thandai (meaning "cold"), a thick, creamy drink blended with nuts, spices, and oat milk. I tasted thandai for the first time in India while celebrating the Holi Festival of Colors with my family. It's an opulent, decadent plant-based milkshake even without dairy ice cream. The thandai masala mixture with spices and nuts is the OG protein powder and can be prepared in advance and kept in the refrigerator for 1 month.

1. **Make the thandai masala:** Combine the almonds, cashews, pistachios, fennel seeds, cardamom, cinnamon, black peppercorns, and nutmeg in a blender or spice grinder. Grind to a fine powder, then set aside.

2. Place the chilled coconut cream in a large bowl. Using a whisk or an electric hand mixer on low speed, whip for about 1 minute, until creamy and smooth and soft peaks form. Use immediately or cover and refrigerate—the whipped cream will harden and set the longer it's chilled, and will keep for up to 2 weeks.

3. **Make the milkshake:** Bloom the saffron threads in a small bowl with 1 tablespoon hot water for 5 minutes. In a blender, combine the oat milk, saffron water, maple syrup, thandai masala, and ice cream and blend until smooth, about 30 seconds.

4. To serve, divide among cups and top with whipped coconut cream and nutmeg.

NOTES

• *Make a simple version using your choice of nuts, cardamom, and cinnamon.*

• *You can use an immersion blender (also called a hand or stick blender) to blend the ingredients in a large bowl or in a widemouthed liquid measuring cup.*

Semolina Halwa

SERVES 4 (½ CUP SERVINGS)

¼ cup pure maple syrup

½ cup semolina flour

½ cup coconut oil

1 teaspoon ground cardamom

Kosher salt

Pinch of saffron threads

1 tablespoon sliced almonds,
  for garnish

1 teaspoon dried rose petals,
  for garnish (optional)

Halwa is a sweet porridge made with semolina flour or lentils. I ate halwa as a toddler and couldn't get enough of it. There are embarrassing stories of me as a child biting my grandmother's shoulder to get a fresh batch of halwa.

Halwa has become synonymous with religious and cultural festivities in India; I always make it for Diwali. The technique for making halwa is very similar to making polenta: add small amounts of liquid at a time and stir constantly for a smooth, consistent texture. The stirring also keeps to a minimum the hot porridge's bursting bubbles, which can splash and burn the cook.

1. Combine the maple syrup with 2 cups water in a small saucepan and heat over medium heat for about 5 minutes. Turn off the heat.

2. Heat a medium Dutch oven or heavy-bottomed pot over medium-low heat. Pour in the semolina flour and coconut oil and stir occasionally until lightly golden, 5 to 7 minutes. Very slowly pour a ladleful of the syrup water into the flour mixture, stirring vigorously to make sure there are no lumps. Continue adding the remaining syrup water in small amounts, stirring constantly after each addition to avoid sticking or burning. Add the cardamom, ½ teaspoon salt, and the saffron and continue stirring until the liquid is absorbed and the mixture resembles polenta, 6 to 8 minutes.

3. Continue to cook until the coconut oil separates slightly from the porridge and the color has turned a darker yellow, about 5 more minutes. Garnish with the sliced almonds and the rose petals (if using). Serve warm, as is traditional, or at room temperature or chilled.

Food Is
JOYFUL

What brings you joy in the world of food?

Exploring new places, finding new ingredients, and learning how to make new recipes are akin to embarking on an exhilarating adventure, where each step is tinged with excitement and a touch of trepidation. Think back to the delight of stumbling upon a hidden restaurant while traveling and venturing into that unknown little side street to experience an unforgettable meal, or discovering an unfamiliar spice blend that you quickly whisked away into your bag to bring home, or triumphantly sharing your joy when your kids love a new recipe you learned to make. The act of exploring, learning, and being a beginner is thrilling, exciting, and intimidating. When we strike the right chord, it's like hitting a high note in a beautiful song. The thrill of such discoveries is unparalleled, a reminder that the world of food is an ever-expansive realm, brimming with limitless possibilities. There's joy in it all.

Leaving my corporate job and going to culinary school was like rekindling a long-lost romance. When I slipped into my chef's coat and stepped into the kitchen, I opened the door to my dreams. With each day and week, I rediscovered the joy that my soul had been craving for years. The culinary school buzzed with a contagious energy, and as I soaked in knowledge and honed my skills, my sense of joy soared. That experience was a journey of self-discovery. Whether it's with food or life, stretching in new directions inevitably leads to discovering joy and a new facet of ourselves.

Date & Tamarind Chutney

MAKES 1½ CUPS

1 cup whole dates, pitted and chopped

⅓ cup tamarind concentrate

½ teaspoon ground fennel

½ teaspoon ground coriander

½ teaspoon ground cumin

½ teaspoon ground ginger

½ tablespoon black salt (kala namak)

⅛ teaspoon ground cayenne

Kosher salt

NOTE: *You can substitute ¼ cup light brown sugar for the dates.*

A sweet and spicy chutney is like the yin and yang of food together in one dish. One fires up the palate and the other sweeps in with sweetness. This chutney is usually served together with Cilantro Chutney (page 4).

1. Combine the chopped dates and tamarind concentrate with 2 cups water in a small saucepan over medium heat. Add the fennel, coriander, cumin, ginger, black salt, and cayenne. Stir to combine. Cook the mixture for about 10 minutes, stirring occasionally, until the dates have cooked down slightly. Season with salt to taste. Remove the chutney from the heat and let it cool to room temperature.

2. Once cooled, transfer the chutney to a blender (or use an immersion blender) and puree until smooth. Serve immediately or store in an airtight container in the refrigerator for up to 1 week.

Garlic Naan

MAKES 8 NAAN

2 cups all-purpose flour, sifted, plus more for the work surface

2 teaspoons kosher salt

1½ teaspoons cane sugar

1 teaspoon double-acting baking powder

¼ teaspoon baking soda

¼ cup plain plant-based yogurt

2 tablespoons neutral oil, plus more for oiling the dough

¼ cup minced garlic (from about 8 large garlic cloves)

Toppings of your choice (such as diced red onion, Thai chilies, cilantro, black sesame seeds, or nigella seeds)

4 tablespoons plant-based butter or coconut oil, melted

Dough making is my practice of presence. Meticulously made and cooked in a blisteringly hot tandoor oven, naan is one of India's best-known breads. When I make naan at home, there's something triumphant and joyful about the whole experience. Because hands and fingers have so many nerves, kneading dough by hand brings me into the present moment, and I prefer this method over using a machine. For this recipe, the naan is cooked on a gas stovetop.

1. Preheat the oven to 200°F.

2. Combine the flour, salt, sugar, baking powder, and baking soda in a medium bowl. Add the yogurt, oil, and ½ cup water and stir until combined. Transfer the dough to a lightly floured work surface and knead until it is smooth and a little less sticky, about 5 minutes. Lightly oil a large bowl, transfer the dough to the oiled bowl, and turn to coat. Cover with a clean kitchen towel and set aside to rest for at least 10 minutes. Lightly oil the dough ball with ½ teaspoon oil, re-cover it, and place in the oven with the light on for 4 hours, or until it has doubled in size.

3. Transfer the dough to a clean work surface dusted with flour and knead the dough again. Divide into 8 equal-size dough balls. Keep them covered while you work with one at a time.

4. Flour a rolling pin and roll out 1 dough ball. Roll away from the center to the edge to make an oblong flatbread as thin (about ⅛ inch) and even as possible without tearing. Sprinkle a small amount (1 to 2 teaspoons) of garlic all over the naan, followed by a small amount of your desired toppings. Use the rolling pin to press the toppings into the dough. Gently flip over the naan and, using your fingers, lightly wet the back side of the naan with a little water.

(recipe continues)

5. Heat a large cast-iron skillet over medium heat for 3 to 5 minutes, until very hot. Place the naan on the hot skillet wet side down and cook for about 2 minutes. You'll see large and small bubbles forming and the crust will become aromatic.

6. Increase the heat to high. Using tongs, carefully grab the naan off the skillet and invert it over the burner directly on top of the fire. Brown the top side of the dough where bubbles have formed, 15 to 20 seconds.

7. Keep the naan warm by wrapping it in a clean kitchen towel and placing it in the oven. Clean and dry the skillet; repeat with the remaining dough. Brush the naan with melted butter and serve hot. Store leftover naan in an airtight container in the refrigerator for up to 2 days. To reheat, place in a 350°F oven for 3 to 5 minutes.

Roasted Chickpeas

MAKES 1¼ CUPS

One 14-ounce can chickpeas, drained and rinsed

2 tablespoons neutral oil

1 teaspoon chaat masala

½ teaspoon ground cumin

½ teaspoon ground coriander

¼ teaspoon paprika

¼ teaspoon kosher salt

Cans of chickpeas are always in my pantry. I cook with the chickpeas and save the canned liquid (aquafaba) for baking (see page xxvii). The snack food aisle at an Indian grocery store has lots of addictive snacks made from chickpea flour, including my go-to, fried black chickpeas dusted with spices (chana chor garam). My roasted chickpeas have that same lip-puckering taste and can be enjoyed as a snack or sprinkled on a salad. Buy canned chickpeas with low sodium to control the salt.

1. Preheat the oven to 400°F.

2. Spread the chickpeas on a microwave-safe plate and pat them dry with a paper towel. Microwave for 3 minutes to dry them out. The exterior should crack a little and they will shrink.

3. Transfer the chickpeas to a medium bowl. Add the oil and toss the chickpeas until well-coated.

4. In a small bowl, mix the chaat masala, cumin, coriander, paprika, and salt. Sprinkle the spice mixture over the chickpeas and toss until evenly coated.

5. Spread the chickpeas in a single layer on a small baking sheet. Roast for 20 to 25 minutes, until crispy and golden brown.

6. Let the chickpeas cool to room temperature before serving. Store in an airtight container in a cool, dry place for up to 3 days.

Tamarind Rasam (Immunity Soup)

MAKES 1 QUART (4 CUPS)

1 tablespoon neutral oil

½ teaspoon black mustard seeds

6 medium Roma (plum) tomatoes, diced

20 curry leaves

2-inch knob fresh ginger, grated (about 1 tablespoon)

1 teaspoon ground turmeric

Kosher salt

¼ teaspoon asafoetida (hing)

3 cups vegetable broth

2 teaspoons tamarind concentrate

2 teaspoons ground coriander

1 teaspoon Kashmiri chili powder

1 teaspoon cane sugar

½ teaspoon ground cumin

2 tablespoons urad dal

2 tablespoons chana dal

Freshly ground black pepper

½ cup chopped fresh cilantro leaves and stems

Throughout the pandemic, I made rasam, a nourishing soup with heaps of immunity-boosting ingredients like ginger, turmeric, and tamarind. Rasam can be made with just tamarind, tomatoes, and spices for a thinner, brothy soup, or with a dried powder made of urad and chana dals to give this soup body and protein.

1. Heat the oil in a large skillet over medium heat until it is shimmering. Add the mustard seeds and cook until they sputter, about 1 minute. Add the tomatoes, curry leaves, ginger, turmeric, 1 teaspoon salt, and the asafoetida. Cook until the tomatoes begin to soften, about 10 minutes. Stir in the vegetable broth, tamarind concentrate, coriander, Kashmiri chili powder, sugar, and cumin and continue cooking for another 10 minutes.

2. Meanwhile, grind the urad and chana dals in a spice grinder to make a fine powder. Whisk the powder into the soup, breaking up any clumps. Season with black pepper, and taste and adjust with additional salt and black pepper if desired. Turn off the heat and stir in the cilantro. Serve hot.

Lentil Lettuce Cups (Khasta Kachoris)

MAKES 16 GENEROUSLY FILLED
LETTUCE CUPS TO SERVE 4

1 cup brown lentils, rinsed

1 cup walnuts

2 tablespoons neutral oil

½-inch knob fresh ginger, grated (about ½ teaspoon)

1 tablespoon dried fenugreek leaves (kasoori methi)

1 tablespoon ground coriander

2 teaspoons ground cumin

½ teaspoon amchur (mango powder)

¼ teaspoon ground turmeric

¼ teaspoon Garam Masala (page xxiii) or store-bought

¼ teaspoon ground cayenne

⅛ teaspoon asafoetida (hing)

¼ cup chopped fresh cilantro

Juice of ½ lime (about 1 tablespoon)

Kosher salt

1 head of butter lettuce, leaves separated

Toppings

Cilantro Chutney (page 4)

Date & Tamarind Chutney (page 62)

Pickled Onions (page 97)

2 medium carrots, thinly shaved or shredded

¼ cup toasted salted pumpkin seeds

Kachoris, a street snack from Gujarat, are deep-fried balls or discs, often filled with lentils, peas, and spices. After catering a huge event at my restaurant, I found myself with extra filling and had an ingenious idea to transform the recipe into a lettuce cup. This adapted recipe has the taste of khasta kachori, without the dough making or frying. I've added walnuts for extra crunchiness and protein.

1. Bring a medium saucepan of water to a boil over medium-high heat. Add the lentils. Reduce the heat to medium and simmer for 25 minutes, or until tender. Drain in a fine-mesh strainer and set aside.

2. Place the walnuts in the bowl of a food chopper and pulse until coarsely chopped. The mixture should resemble crumbles; do not puree.

3. Heat the oil in a large skillet over medium-low heat until it is shimmering. Add the lentils and walnuts, then stir in the ginger, fenugreek leaves, coriander, cumin, amchur, turmeric, garam masala, cayenne, and asafoetida. Stir to combine. Increase the heat to medium and cook until the filling is heated through, 5 to 7 minutes. Remove from the heat. Stir in the cilantro and lime juice. Season with salt to taste.

4. Serve ¼ cup filling in each lettuce cup with the toppings alongside.

Herbed Lentil Soup

SERVES 4 TO 6

1 cup Puy lentils, rinsed

⅛ teaspoon saffron threads

2 tablespoons neutral oil

1 medium yellow onion, thinly sliced

5 or 6 scallions, white and light green parts, thinly sliced

Kosher salt and freshly ground black pepper

2 garlic cloves, minced

1½ teaspoons ground turmeric

1 large sweet potato, peeled and cut into ½-inch cubes (about 2 cups)

1 quart (4 cups) vegetable broth

½ cup tightly packed chopped fresh parsley

½ cup tightly packed chopped fresh dill

Juice of 1 lemon (about 2 tablespoons)

NOTES

• *Soaking the lentils reduces the cooking time.*

• *If you don't have vegetable broth, use two low-sodium vegetable bouillon cubes mixed with 4 cups warm water.*

This soup is adapted from a popular Iranian herb stew called ghormeh sabzi, which is made from mountains of herbs. In my simpler version, I keep most of the vibrant green herbs while adding Puy lentils and sweet potatoes to make the dish heartier. The richness is enhanced by saffron, and the scent of the herbs fills the entire home while the stew simmers. If you love any herb more than another in this recipe, just adjust the quantity to your liking. Swapping butternut squash for the sweet potato works well too.

1. Place the lentils in a small bowl and add warm water to cover. In a separate small bowl, combine the saffron with 1 tablespoon warm water. Set both bowls aside.

2. Heat the oil in a large Dutch oven over medium-high heat until it is shimmering. Add the onion, scallions, and 1 teaspoon each salt and pepper. Sauté, stirring frequently, until the onion is translucent, 5 to 6 minutes. Stir in the garlic, turmeric, and saffron water and cook for 30 seconds.

3. Drain the lentils, discarding the soaking liquid. Add the lentils, sweet potato, and vegetable broth to the Dutch oven and season with salt to taste. Bring to a boil. Cover, reduce the heat to low, and simmer until the lentils are completely cooked and the sweet potato is tender, about 30 minutes.

4. Remove from the heat and stir in the parsley, dill, and lemon juice; let sit to infuse with the herbs, about 5 minutes. Taste and adjust the seasoning as desired. Serve hot.

Sweet Corn Chowder

SERVES 4 TO 6

⅓ cup old-fashioned rolled oats

8 ears sweet white or yellow corn, shucked, or two 10-ounce packages frozen sweet corn (you will need 4 cups kernels)

2 tablespoons olive oil

1 teaspoon cumin seeds

1 medium yellow onion, chopped

3 scallions, whites and greens, chopped separately

3 garlic cloves, minced

Kosher salt

½ teaspoon paprika

1 teaspoon ground turmeric

1 teaspoon ground coriander

¼ teaspoon ground cayenne

Freshly ground black pepper

½ cup plain plant-based yogurt

1 teaspoon fresh lemon juice

I had this corn soup at a dinner party in Saudi Arabia. The host made it with freshly picked sweet corn from her farm. Its creamy consistency comes from pureed oatmeal! I was delighted to see how quickly oatmeal thickens a soup. The sourness from the yogurt and lemon juice balances the sweetness of the corn and oatmeal.

1. Combine the oats and 2 cups water in a medium bowl. Set aside to hydrate.

2. Meanwhile, cut the kernels from the corn: Stand a corn cob on its end on a cutting board and firmly slice downward with a knife to remove the kernels. Scoop the kernels into a medium bowl. Repeat with the remaining ears of corn.

3. Transfer the soaked oats with their liquid to a blender. Puree on high speed until a thick puree forms, about 1 minute.

4. Heat the oil in a Dutch oven over medium heat. Add the cumin seeds and cook until they sputter, about 30 seconds. Add the onion, scallion whites, garlic, and 1 teaspoon salt. Cook until softened and translucent, 3 to 5 minutes. Stir in the paprika, turmeric, coriander, and cayenne and season with black pepper. Sauté until aromatic, about 2 minutes. Stir in the reserved corn kernels, oat puree, and yogurt with 4 cups water.

5. Increase the heat to medium-high and bring the liquid to a boil, then reduce the heat to medium-low, cover, and simmer, stirring occasionally to keep the oatmeal from sticking, until the soup is slightly thickened, 25 to 30 minutes. For a thicker consistency, continue to cook uncovered for another 5 to 7 minutes.

6. Remove from the heat. Stir in the lemon juice and adjust the consistency and seasoning as needed. Serve immediately.

Palak Paneer

SERVES 4

Masala

1 medium yellow onion, roughly chopped

5 garlic cloves, peeled

1 Thai chili

¼-inch knob fresh ginger

¼ bunch fresh cilantro

4 to 6 raw cashews

3 green cardamom pods

One 1-inch cinnamon stick, or ½ teaspoon ground cinnamon

5 black peppercorns, or ¼ teaspoon freshly ground black pepper

2 whole cloves, or ⅛ teaspoon ground cloves

2 tablespoons unsweetened shredded coconut

Spinach Gravy

5 medium ripe Roma (plum) tomatoes, quartered

¼ cup neutral oil

8 ounces super-firm tofu, patted dry with a towel and cut into ½-inch cubes

1½ tablespoons golden raisins

5 raw cashews

½ teaspoon baking soda

1 pound fresh spinach

Kosher salt

In Hindi "palak" means one of two things, depending on how it is pronounced: *pa-luck* versus *puhluck*. The first pronunciation is the dish, palak (pa-luck) paneer. The second pronunciation (puhluck) means "eyelashes," which happens to be my name. This classic recipe uses lots of fresh palak (spinach) for that eye-popping green color. The sautéed masala is essential to re-creating a restaurant-style version at home.

1. **Make the masala:** Combine all the masala ingredients in a blender and puree until a smooth paste forms. Transfer the masala to a small bowl and set aside. Do not clean the blender.

2. **Make the spinach gravy:** Place the chopped tomatoes in the blender and puree on high speed until smooth. Do not clean the blender.

3. In a heavy-bottomed saucepan, heat 2 tablespoons of the oil over medium heat. Add the tofu and sauté until golden brown all over, about 10 minutes. Transfer to a plate and set aside.

4. Heat the remaining 2 tablespoons oil. Add the masala, raisins, and cashews and cook until fragrant, 7 to 10 minutes. Add the tomato puree and cook for another 15 minutes.

5. Meanwhile, bring a large pot of water to a boil and add the baking soda. Fill a large bowl with ice water. Blanch the spinach in the boiling water for 10 to 15 seconds, then immediately transfer to the cold water to stop the cooking. Drain the spinach and transfer it to the blender. Puree until very smooth, about 1 minute.

6. Add the spinach puree and tofu to the saucepan, heat through, and season with salt to taste. Serve immediately with naan or rice.

Vegetable Dal Stew with Tomatoes

SERVES 6 TO 8

Vegetable Dal

2 tablespoons neutral oil

2 teaspoons cumin seeds

1 medium butternut squash, peeled, seeded, and cut into ½-inch dice (about 2 cups)

1 medium yellow onion, chopped

1 medium carrot, cut into ¼-inch dice

Kosher salt

2 tablespoons tomato paste

2 garlic cloves, minced

2-inch knob fresh ginger, grated (about 1 tablespoon)

1 teaspoon ground turmeric

1 teaspoon Garam Masala (page xxiii) or store-bought

½ teaspoon ground cayenne

½ teaspoon freshly ground black pepper, plus more as needed

One 15-ounce can chickpeas, rinsed and drained

1 cup masoor dal, rinsed

6 cups vegetable broth

1 bunch of rainbow chard, finely chopped (about 4 cups)

Juice of ½ lemon (about 1 tablespoon)

Stewed Tomatoes

1 tablespoon neutral oil

½ teaspoon cumin seeds

1 pint cherry tomatoes

Kosher salt

When *Forbes* asked me for tips on eating well, I immediately offered this recipe, which is a stew filled with vegetables and dal. My version of a one-pot vegetable dal—an easy weeknight meal—is a play on a traditional recipe to incorporate more vegetables and greens. This stew is packed with protein and fiber. I love adding stewed tomatoes for a pop of color on top, versus cooking them down in the recipe.

1. **Make the vegetable dal:** Heat the oil in a large Dutch oven over medium heat until it is shimmering. Add the cumin seeds and cook until they sputter, about 30 seconds. Stir in the squash, onion, carrot, and 1 teaspoon salt and cook, stirring occasionally, until the vegetables have softened, 10 to 12 minutes.

2. Stir in the tomato paste, garlic, ginger, turmeric, garam masala, cayenne, ½ teaspoon salt, and the black pepper and cook until fragrant, about 1 minute. Stir in the chickpeas, dal, and broth.

3. Cover the pot and simmer over medium-low heat, stirring occasionally, for about 1 hour, until the squash is tender and the dal is soft.

4. **Make the stewed tomatoes:** Heat the oil in a medium skillet over medium-high heat until it is shimmering. Add the cumin seeds and cook until they sputter, about 30 seconds. Add the tomatoes and season with salt to taste; cook until the tomatoes have softened, 5 to 7 minutes. Transfer to a bowl and set aside.

5. Remove the Dutch oven from the heat, stir in the chard, and leave covered for 10 minutes. Remove the lid, taste, and season with more salt and black pepper if desired. Stir in the lemon juice and serve hot, topped with the stewed tomatoes.

Peach-Cardamom Buttermilk Cake

MAKES ONE 9-INCH CAKE

One 10-ounce bag frozen sliced peaches

2 lemons

¾ cup plain soy or other plant-based milk

2 tablespoons ground flaxseed

1⅓ cups plus 1 tablespoon fine semolina flour

⅓ cup all-purpose flour

¼ teaspoon kosher salt

¾ cup plus 2 tablespoons cane sugar

1 teaspoon ground cardamom

2 teaspoons ground fennel

⅓ cup neutral oil, plus more for greasing

1½ teaspoons baking powder

¼ teaspoon baking soda

When Georgia peaches are in season, they are on repeat for summer recipes. I've developed this recipe using frozen peaches so this buttermilk cake can be enjoyed year-round. The spongy texture and pop of cardamom will greet your mouth with a minty kiss.

1. Place an oven rack in the middle position and preheat the oven to 350°F. Grease a 9-inch springform cake pan or line a round quiche pan with parchment paper.

2. Divide the frozen peaches in half. Chop half of the peaches into small pieces for the batter, place them in a small bowl, and set aside. Reserve the whole slices for the topping. In a small bowl, zest both lemons and set aside.

3. To make a nondairy buttermilk, pour the soy milk into a measuring cup and squeeze in the lemon juice (the lemons should yield about ¼ cup juice). Let sit until curdled, 5 to 10 minutes. Meanwhile, in a small bowl, combine the flaxseed with 6 tablespoons water.

4. Place the semolina flour, all-purpose flour, salt, sugar, cardamom, and fennel in a large bowl and whisk to combine. Add the oil, buttermilk, flaxseed mixture, and lemon zest. Whisk until no lumps remain. Whisk the baking powder and baking soda into the batter and fold in the chopped peaches.

5. If using a quiche pan, arrange the sliced peaches on the bottom, then pour the batter over the top (you'll invert the cake after baking). Otherwise, pour the batter into the prepared springform cake pan, spread evenly, and arrange the sliced peaches on top of the batter. Bake until the cake is firm to the touch and a knife inserted into the center comes out clean, about 45 minutes. Cool completely and unmold from the springform pan or invert the quiche pan before serving.

Food Is
COMFORT

What is your comfort food?

Soup, grilled cheese, or a cozy bowl of curry are the foods that I turn to when I'm feeling down, stressed, or homesick. Maybe for you it's a special recipe your mom made, your grandma's cooking, or your favorite childhood snack. Whatever it is, there's no denying that comfort foods have a way of making everything better. They remind us of happy times with family and friends, of cozy nights in front of a fire, or of carefree moments in our lives.

But why do we crave these foods so much? Yes, they have satisfying tastes and textures. But it's also because of the emotional connection we have to them. Whatever the reason may be, comfort food has a particular significance in my heart (and stomach). So the next time you eat your go-to comfort food, stop and savor each bite. Sometimes a little comfort food is all you need to feel better.

Garlic-Sesame Chili Oil

MAKES 1¼ CUPS

2 tablespoons white
    sesame seeds

1 tablespoon black
    sesame seeds

2 teaspoons onion powder

2 teaspoons garlic powder

2 tablespoons Kashmiri chili
    powder

1½ teaspoons amchur (mango
    powder)

½ tablespoon pink
    Himalayan salt

1 cup neutral oil

A good chili oil is as important as salt in my kitchen. This one gets its smoky and sour kick from the amchur and bright red color from the Kashmiri chili powder. It's a condiment that can perk up a lot of dishes; it's always in my fridge. The nutty and toasty notes of sesame seeds with the fiery kick of chili will have your taste buds dancing. I find ways to sneak in a spoonful every day—using it as a dipping sauce with bread and drizzling it on pretty much anything.

1. Combine the white and black sesame seeds, onion powder, garlic powder, Kashmiri chili powder, amchur, and salt in a small heat-proof bowl.

2. Heat the oil in a heavy-bottomed saucepan over medium-high heat for 3 to 5 minutes, until its surface has a sheen (but it should not be smoky). Carefully pour the hot oil over the spices and whisk to combine. Let cool completely. Store the oil in an airtight jar in the refrigerator for up to 2 months. Stir the oil with a spoon before using.

NOTE: *Substitute Kashmiri chili powder with paprika (for color) and crushed red pepper flakes (for heat) in equal parts.*

Tomato Chutney

MAKES 1 CUP

1 tablespoon neutral oil

1 teaspoon cumin seeds

2 tablespoons chana dal, toor dal, or yellow moong dal

3 medium Roma (plum) tomatoes, diced

1 small yellow onion, chopped

½-inch knob fresh ginger, chopped (about ½ teaspoon)

1 teaspoon tamarind concentrate, or 1 tablespoon lemon juice

¼ teaspoon ground cayenne

⅛ teaspoon asafoetida (hing)

Kosher salt

South Indian tomato chutney is very distinct because the cooked-down tomatoes become creamy from the pureed dal. This smooth tomato chutney is always served with dosa, idli, and uttapam.

Heat the oil in a medium skillet over medium heat until it is shimmering. Add the cumin seeds and cook until they sputter, about 30 seconds. Add the chana dal and cook for 3 to 4 minutes. Add the tomatoes, onion, ginger, tamarind, cayenne, and asafoetida. Season with salt to taste and cook until the onion is softened and translucent, another 5 to 7 minutes. Transfer the chutney to a blender and puree until smooth. Store in an airtight container in the refrigerator for up to 1 week.

Background: Tomato Chutney (page 87);
foreground: Coconut Chutney (opposite)

Coconut Chutney

MAKES 2 CUPS

2 cups grated fresh coconut (see Notes)

½ cup raw cashews or roasted chana dal (see Notes)

½-inch knob fresh ginger

1 Thai or serrano chili

Juice of ½ lime (about 1 tablespoon)

Kosher salt

Tadka

1 tablespoon neutral oil

½ teaspoon black mustard seeds

½ teaspoon urad dal

1 to 2 whole dried red chilies (optional)

5 curry leaves

Coconut chutney is a South Indian condiment served at breakfast with dosa and idli. Make this chutney with whole brown coconut or dried or frozen unsweetened coconut. I've recently started seeing whole coconuts at my local grocery store and I couldn't be happier. Smashing the coconut in my backyard is part of the fun in making this recipe. Serve this and Tomato Chutney (page 87) with Uttapam (page 103).

1. Blend the coconut, cashews, ginger, chili, lime juice, 1 teaspoon salt, and ½ cup water in a high-speed blender until a smooth paste forms. Taste and add more salt if needed. Transfer the chutney to a small bowl.

2. **Make the tadka:** Heat the oil in a small saucepan over medium heat. Add the mustard seeds, urad dal, and dried red chilies (if using). Cook until the mustard seeds start to pop and the urad dal turns golden brown, about 1 minute.

3. Add the curry leaves and stir for a few seconds. Pour the tadka over the chutney and mix well. Store the chutney in an airtight container in the refrigerator for up to 1 week.

NOTES

• You can substitute frozen coconut or unsweetened dry coconut flakes for the fresh. Add more water, a tablespoon at a time, to achieve a creamier consistency.

• Traditional recipes are made with dried chana dal, but I like cashews.

Mint Masala Popcorn

SERVES 4

½ teaspoon Dried Mint
(page 17)

½ teaspoon ground coriander

¼ teaspoon ground cayenne

½ teaspoon Garam Masala
(page xxiii) or store-bought

2 tablespoons
nutritional yeast

1 tablespoon amchur (mango
powder)

½ teaspoon Spicewell pepper
blend, or ¼ teaspoon
turmeric plus ¼ teaspoon
ground black pepper

4 tablespoons plant-based
butter

3 tablespoons neutral oil

½ cup popcorn kernels

Kosher salt

A budget-friendly, easy snack, stovetop popcorn is a no-brainer. Ditch those prepackaged salty ones and make your own masala popcorn. This one, with mint and amchur, is mixed with spices to give it a kick. It's my pick-me-up snack when I need an afternoon crunchy treat or a late-night bite.

1. Combine all the spices in a small bowl. In a separate small bowl or measuring cup, microwave the butter for 30 seconds, or until melted.

2. Heat the oil in a large heavy-bottomed saucepan with a tight-fitting lid over medium heat until it is shimmering. Add the popcorn kernels, stir, and cover the pan. Listen for a popping sound, then shake the pan a little to distribute the kernels evenly. Once the kernels start popping faster, open the lid just a touch to allow the steam to escape. Continue cooking until the popping sound subsides.

3. Remove the lid and pour the popcorn into a large bowl. Drizzle with half the melted butter and sprinkle on half the spice mix and toss to combine. Add the remaining butter and spice mix, toss again, season with salt to taste, and serve immediately.

Tomato Soup (Shorba)

SERVES 2 TO 4

1 bunch fresh cilantro, stems and leaves separated

8 medium Roma (plum) tomatoes, quartered

1 medium carrot, chopped

1-inch knob fresh ginger, chopped (about 1 teaspoon)

1 teaspoon ground coriander

1 teaspoon cumin seeds

¼ teaspoon ground cardamom

¼ teaspoon Garam Masala (page xxiii) or store-bought

⅛ teaspoon ground turmeric

⅛ teaspoon ground cayenne

Kosher salt and freshly ground black pepper

2 cups vegetable broth or water

Store-bought croutons, for garnish

Soup is universally known as a comfort food. It's warm, soothing, and nourishing and a sign of care when made for someone you love. Whether it's hearty, spicy, or creamy, every culture has a soup. Tomato shorba is India's comfort soup, with two different pops of freshness from cilantro stems and cardamom. My mom would make this tomato soup for me after school, and I always thought of it as a hug in a bowl from her.

1. Combine the cilantro stems, tomatoes, carrot, ginger, coriander, cumin, cardamom, garam masala, turmeric, cayenne, ½ teaspoon salt, ½ teaspoon black pepper, and the vegetable broth in a high-speed blender and puree on high until smooth.

2. Transfer the tomato puree to a large saucepan and simmer for about 20 minutes to cook the tomatoes and incorporate the flavors. Taste and add more salt and black pepper if needed. Serve the soup garnished with the croutons.

NOTE: *You can make this soup in a high-speed blender by adding all the ingredients, except the croutons, and pureeing them on high for 10 minutes. The blender heats and cooks the soup.*

Seekh Kebab Burger & Plantain Chips

MAKES 4 BURGERS

1 pound Beyond Burger meat, thawed

½ small yellow onion, grated

2 Thai chilies, minced

2 garlic cloves, minced

1-inch knob fresh ginger, grated (about 1 teaspoon)

1 teaspoon ground cumin

2 teaspoons ground coriander

2 teaspoons amchur (mango powder)

½ teaspoon Garam Masala (page xxiii) or store-bought

1 teaspoon kosher salt

Neutral oil, for cooking

4 burger buns, split in half, lightly toasted

¼ cup plant-based mayonnaise

Pickled Onions (page 97)

4 leaves butter lettuce

Plantain Chips (recipe follows on page 96)

When I'm invited to a barbecue, I'm relegated to eating premade veggie burgers. At my restaurant Dash & Chutney, I added a Beyond meat burger to the menu seasoned with spices to mimic Indian seekh kebabs that are made with minced meat. This vegan burger stays extra juicy after cooking from the grated onions. Serve with plantain chips.

1. In a large bowl, mix together the burger meat, onion, chilies, garlic, ginger, cumin, coriander, amchur, garam masala, and salt. Divide evenly into 4 patties.

2. Heat a few drops of oil in a large skillet or a grill pan over medium-high heat and evenly sear the patties for 2 minutes on each side. Serve the burger patties on the toasted buns spread with the mayonnaise, topped with the pickled onions and lettuce, with plantain chips on the side.

NOTE: *You can make these burgers ahead of time and freeze the uncooked patties for up to a month. Thaw them in the refrigerator for 4 hours before cooking.*

Plantain Chips

SERVES 4
2 large unripened green
   plantains
Neutral oil, for frying
Kosher salt

NOTES

*• Don't overcrowd
the pan when frying
the plantains or the
temperature of the
oil will drop and the
plantains will not cook
evenly. If the plantains
start to brown too
quickly, reduce the
heat to medium-low.*

*• AIR FRYER COOKING:
Add the plantains
to a bowl with
2 tablespoons oil and
salt. Working in small
batches, bake at 350°F
for 5 to 7 minutes,
tossing the plantains
once or twice during
cooking.*

These chips are a popular snack made from unripened plantains, which are a starchy cousin of the banana. Plantains can be eaten at different stages of ripeness, and the ripeness will affect the flavor and texture of the chips.

Green plantains are unripe and have a starchy interior. When fried or baked, they become crispy and have a nutty taste. Yellow plantains are ripe and have a sweeter flavor. When fried or baked, they become soft and chewy.

1. Cut the tops and bottoms off the plantains. Using a paring knife, run the tip lengthwise down each plantain to score the skin without cutting into the flesh. Firmly push the peel away from the flesh—the peel may come off in sections.

2. Using a mandoline or a knife, cut the plantains into thin rounds, about ⅛ inch thick.

3. In a Dutch oven or a heavy-bottomed pan, heat 2 inches of oil over medium heat to 350°F.

4. Add the plantain slices to the hot oil and cook for 2 to 3 minutes per side, until golden and crispy. Remove the plantains from the oil and place on a paper towel–lined plate. Season immediately with salt to taste, while they are still hot.

Pickled Onions

MAKES 1 CUP

1 medium red onion, halved and sliced ⅛ inch thick

1 cup white vinegar

⅓ cup cane sugar

1 teaspoon kosher salt

1 tablespoon coriander seeds

1 teaspoon black peppercorns

Pickled onions are simple and quick to make but offer so much to any dish. The acidic and sweet onion flavor is always a complement to a finished dish. Coriander seeds and black peppercorns make these pickled onions extra punchy.

1. Pack the thinly sliced onions into a quart-size mason jar or other heat-proof container.

2. In a small saucepan, combine the vinegar, sugar, salt, coriander seeds, and black peppercorns. Bring to a boil over medium-high heat, stirring until the sugar and salt have dissolved. Remove the saucepan from the heat and let the mixture cool for a few minutes.

3. Carefully pour the hot pickling liquid over the onions. Let the onions cool completely, about 30 minutes. Cover and place in the refrigerator. Let them sit for at least 1 hour before using or, for best results, leave the pickled onions in the refrigerator for 24 hours before consuming. Store in the refrigerator for up to 3 weeks.

Mumbai Grilled Cheese

MAKES 2 SANDWICHES

4 slices of bread, preferably sourdough

2 tabespoons plant-based mayonnaise

2 tablespoons Cilantro Chutney (page 4)

2 tablespoons Indian Ketchup (Kasundi) (page 37)

4 slices plant-based cheese, such as Field Roast Chao Cheese

½ small green bell pepper, cored, seeded, and cut into rings

1 medium Roma (plum) tomato, thinly sliced

½ small red onion, cut into thin rings

1 small cooked peeled potato, sliced into ⅛-inch rounds

1 teaspoon chaat masala

Grilled cheese is a popular street food in the bustling city of Mumbai. This iconic sandwich is made with chutneys, spices, vegetables, and cheese. Simply watching the showmanship of each small cart or stall owner whets the appetite and adds to the charm and excitement.

1. Heat a large skillet or grill pan over medium heat.

2. Place the bread on a cutting board and smear the mayonnaise on one side of each slice.

3. On the opposite side of two of the slices, with the mayo side down, spread 1 tablespoon each of the chutney and the Indian ketchup. Place 2 slices of the cheese on top of the ketchup, then layer the vegetables on top of the cheese. Sprinkle the chaat masala over both slices, then carefully close the sandwiches with the remaining 2 slices of bread.

4. Place the sandwiches on the skillet and cook, covered, until the bread is golden brown and the cheese is melted, 2 to 3 minutes on each side. When you flip the sandwiches, press down on them with a spatula to help compress and melt the cheese (see Notes).

NOTES

• While traditional recipes use butter on the exterior of the bread, I smear a thin layer of mayonnaise instead. This ensures the bread has an even golden exterior and extra crunch.

• Plant-based (vegan) cheese will not melt completely because it lacks casein, the protein that causes regular dairy cheese to melt.

My Beat Bobby Flay Chik'n Curry

SERVES 4 TO 6

Masala

4 cardamom pods

4 whole cloves

1 tablespoon cumin seeds

1 teaspoon coriander seeds

1 teaspoon fennel seeds

¼ teaspoon black peppercorns

Vegan Chicken Curry

3 tablespoons neutral oil

Two 8-ounce packages plant-based chicken, such as Daring Original Plant Chicken, defrosted and cut into ½-inch pieces

2 large yellow onions, chopped (about 3 cups)

2 Thai chilies, chopped

3 or 4 garlic cloves, minced

2-inch knob fresh ginger, finely chopped (about 1 tablespoon)

4 medium Roma (plum) tomatoes

2 bay leaves

One 1½-inch cinnamon stick

⅛ teaspoon asafoetida (hing)

1 teaspoon cane sugar

½ teaspoon ground cayenne

¼ teaspoon ground turmeric

Kosher salt

¼ cup coconut milk

Cumin rice (see Notes on page 11), for serving

This is the Beat Bobby Flay chicken curry, for which I'm most known. The proudest moment in my culinary life that also made me famous across America. This plant-based curry is still just as dynamite as the original winning dish. There's no substitute for the depth that toasted whole spices add to the sauce, and taking the time for this step is what helped me lock in a win. Rewatching the show with my grandmother before she passed away, I beamed with pride that she could watch me on television beating an Iron Chef making Indian food.

1. **Make the masala:** In a 10-inch dry skillet over medium heat, toast the cardamom pods, cloves, cumin seeds, coriander seeds, fennel seeds, and black peppercorns until aromatic, about 5 minutes. Let them cool, then transfer the toasted spices to a spice grinder, a mortar with pestle, or a small blender. Grind them into a fine powder. Set aside.

2. **Make the vegan chicken curry:** Heat 1 tablespoon of the oil in a Dutch oven or large heavy-bottomed pot over medium heat. Add the plant chicken and 3 tablespoons water and sauté until lightly golden and the water has evaporated, 3 to 5 minutes. Remove the chicken from the pot and set aside. Wipe the Dutch oven clean with a paper towel.

3. Place the onions, Thai chilies, garlic, and ginger in a blender, add 1 or 2 tablespoons water, and puree on high until smooth, about 1 minute. Transfer the onion puree to a medium bowl, then add the tomatoes to the blender and puree on high for 1 minute. Set the blender aside. In the same Dutch oven, heat the remaining 2 tablespoons oil over medium heat. Add the onion mixture, bay leaves, cinnamon stick, and asafoetida and cook, stirring occasionally, until the mixture is a light caramel color, 15 to 20 minutes. The onions will reduce as their water evaporates.

(recipe continues)

4. Add the pureed tomatoes to the onion mixture and cook for another 10 minutes. Stir in the sugar, cayenne, and turmeric. Add the cooked chicken, toasted spice masala, and 1 teaspoon salt. Reduce the heat to medium-low and cook, stirring occasionally, until the tomatoes begin to turn into a smooth, loose paste and the oil begins to separate and appear on top of the mixture. Cover and continue to cook, stirring occasionally, for about 20 minutes more. Stir in the coconut milk. Adjust the seasoning with more salt if needed. Keep warm until ready to serve, and serve with cumin rice.

Uttapam

1¼ cups white rice

¼ cup urad dal

2 tablespoons chana dal

¼ teaspoon fenugreek seeds (methi)

1 teaspoon kosher salt

1 red onion, finely chopped

1 medium Roma (plum) tomato, diced

1 Thai chili, or ½ serrano chili, chopped

1 medium carrot, grated

¼ cup chopped fresh cilantro leaves

Neutral oil, for cooking

Coconut Chutney (page 89) and Tomato Chutney (page 87), for serving

NOTE: *Indian retailers sell dry packaged idli mix or premade idli batter, which can help cut down prep time.*

Uttapam is a loaded savory pancake. Traditional uttapam is a popular South Indian dish made with leftover fermented rice and dal dosa batter and topped with onions, tomatoes, and masala powder. The thick and fluffy pancake, made without a leavening agent, is crispy on the outside and spongy in the middle. Uttapam and dosa have the same batter recipe. The fermented batter is rich in probiotics and has a sour smell. Loaded with veggies, it's a gratifying breakfast or brunch dish. The rice and dals must soak overnight before making the batter, and then the batter, too, will need to ferment overnight before making the uttapam (see Note). Plan accordingly!

1. Rinse the rice, urad dal, and chana dal in cold water. Transfer to a medium bowl, add water to cover, and let soak overnight. Place the fenugreek seeds in a small bowl, cover with water, and let soak overnight.

2. The next day, drain the water from the rice and dal mixture and the fenugreek seeds and transfer them to a high-speed blender. Blend until smooth, 1 to 2 minutes, adding 1 tablespoon water as needed and pausing to scrape down the sides occasionally. The batter should be smooth and thick in consistency.

3. Transfer the batter to a large bowl, cover with a plate, and drape a clean kitchen towel over the bowl. Let the batter ferment overnight. (In warmer months, it can be left to ferment for as little as 8 hours; but in cooler months, it may ferment up to 24 hours.) You can put it in the oven with the light turned on to expedite fermentation. The batter is fermented when there is condensation on the lid, small air bubbles have formed on the surface, there's a distinct sour smell, and the batter has doubled in volume. Stir the salt into the fermented batter and mix well.

(recipe continues)

4. Heat a large nonstick skillet over medium heat. Working in batches, pour a ladleful of the batter into the skillet and spread it out in a circular motion to form a thick pancake. Reduce the heat and sprinkle some onion, tomato, chili, carrot, and cilantro on top of the batter. Gently press them in with the back of the spatula.

5. Drizzle a few drops of oil on top and around the edges of the uttapam. Cook over low to medium heat until the edges start to turn light brown and crispy and the surface is covered with small air bubbles that have popped, about 3 minutes. Flip the uttapam over and cook for another 2 minutes. Keep the cooked uttapams warm by covering them with a clean kitchen towel and placing them in a 200°F oven. Repeat with the remaining batter.

6. Serve hot with coconut chutney and tomato chutney.

Turmeric Milk (Doodh)

MAKES 2 SERVINGS

2 cups barista-style plain plant-based milk

1 teaspoon Turmeric Paste (recipe follows)

2 teaspoons pure maple syrup, or other sweetener, to taste

Ground cinnamon, for topping

Freshly ground black pepper, for topping

Before turmeric lattes, there was turmeric milk (doodh), also known as golden milk, a traditional Ayurvedic drink made with whole milk and turmeric, used for centuries in India as a home remedy. Turmeric, which has an active compound called curcumin, is an anti-inflammatory and aids in digestion, but it is absorbed by the body only when it is paired with black pepper and a fat. This cozy bright yellow concoction helps calm the body and mind.

Heat the plant-based milk in a small saucepan over low heat until it begins to steam. Whisk in the turmeric paste until well combined. Whisk in the maple syrup and continue heating the milk over low heat until warmed through, 2 to 3 minutes. Remove from the heat. Serve with cinnamon and pepper sprinkled on top.

> NOTE: *If using ground turmeric instead of turmeric paste, substitute ¼ teaspoon ground turmeric and ⅛ teaspoon ground black pepper for the paste. Serve sprinkled with cinnamon and freshly ground black pepper.*

Turmeric Paste

MAKES 1 CUP

4 ounces fresh turmeric root, scrubbed and roughly chopped (about 1 cup)

4-inch knob fresh ginger, roughly chopped (about ¼ cup)

¼ cup coconut oil

2 teaspoons freshly ground black pepper

1 teaspoon ground cinnamon

1. Place the chopped turmeric and ginger and ½ cup water in a high-speed blender or the bowl of a food processor or blender and puree until smooth, 1 to 2 minutes.

2. Transfer the turmeric puree to a small saucepan over low heat. Add the coconut oil and pepper. Cook, stirring occasionally, until the mixture thickens to a paste-like consistency, 10 to 15 minutes.

3. Let the mixture cool to room temperature. Transfer the turmeric paste to a clean jar with a tight-fitting lid and store in the refrigerator for up to 1 month. You may also freeze any extra paste in ice cube trays for adding to any recipe that calls for turmeric and black pepper.

Chocolate-Sesame Banana Bread

MAKES ONE 9-INCH LOAF

Cooking spray

2 cups all-purpose flour

1 teaspoon baking powder

1 teaspoon baking soda

1 teaspoon ground cardamom

½ teaspoon ground cinnamon

⅛ teaspoon freshly grated nutmeg

1 teaspoon kosher salt

½ cup coconut oil

1 cup raw pecans, finely chopped

2 tablespoons ground flaxseed or whole chia seeds

4 small ripe bananas, mashed (1½ cups)

¼ cup applesauce

½ cup firmly packed light or dark brown sugar

¼ cup tahini

6 tablespoons plain oat milk

1 teaspoon pure vanilla extract

⅓ cup vegan dark chocolate chips

1 tablespoon white sesame seeds

While banana bread is not entirely Indian, I like finding ways to use all my pantry staples. I deviate from the classic banana bread recipe by adding sesame seeds and tahini to bring forward more sesame flavor, along with pecans browned in coconut oil. The riper the bananas, the sweeter and more flavorful the bread will be.

1. Place an oven rack in the upper-middle position and preheat the oven to 350°F. Line a 9 × 5-inch loaf pan with parchment paper overhanging by 2 inches on the long sides. Spray with cooking spray. Set aside.

2. Whisk together the flour, baking powder, baking soda, cardamom, cinnamon, nutmeg, and salt in a large bowl.

3. Melt the coconut oil in a medium skillet over medium-low heat. Add the pecans and cook, stirring often with a silicone spatula, until the nuts are amber-colored, 10 to 12 minutes.

4. In a small bowl, combine the flaxseed with 6 tablespoons water; let sit while the pecans are cooking.

5. Transfer the cooked pecans to a separate large bowl, add the bananas, applesauce, brown sugar, tahini, oat milk, vanilla, and flaxseed mixture, and whisk vigorously until smooth.

6. Fold the banana mixture and chocolate chips into the flour mixture until just combined. Transfer the batter to the prepared loaf pan. Sprinkle the sesame seeds over the top.

7. Bake until browned and a toothpick inserted in the center comes out clean, about 50 minutes, rotating the loaf halfway through.

8. Cool the bread in the pan on a wire rack for 10 minutes, then turn out the loaf to cool completely before serving.

Masala Mule

MAKES 4 COCKTAILS
1 cup Masala Syrup (recipe follows)

1 cup lime juice (from about 8 limes)

1 cup bourbon

Ice

1 cup ginger beer

Orange twists, for garnish

Mint sprigs, for garnish

A masala mule is a nod to ingredients once traded along the old spice routes in India and Sri Lanka. Spiced with garam masala and sweetened with maple syrup, this surprising drink can also be made without the bourbon if your guests prefer a mocktail (see Note).

In a large pitcher, stir together the masala syrup, lime juice, and bourbon. Fill four highball glasses with ice and pour the cocktail mixture over, leaving room for the ginger beer. Top off each glass with a few splashes of ginger beer. Garnish with orange twists and mint and serve.

NOTE: *To make a nonalcoholic version of this drink, increase the masala syrup and lime juice by ¼ cup each and top with 3 ounces (¼ cup plus 2 tablespoons) ginger beer.*

Masala Syrup

MAKES 1 CUP
½ cup pure maple syrup

½ tablespoon Garam Masala (page xxiii) or store-bought

Whisk together the maple syrup, garam masala, and ½ cup hot water in a pitcher. Cool completely. Store in a glass jar for up to a week.

Food Is
VIBRANT

What produce colors are you enamored with?

Colorful produce and fruits are an edible offering from nature. A rainbow of colors dances before our eyes at the produce aisle, a kaleidoscope of textures and shapes waiting to be explored. The vibrant red of a sun-ripened tomato, the verdant green of freshly picked herbs, the burgundy gloss of cherries, and the gold of sweet corn—all nature's gift to us. To truly appreciate this gift, pause for a moment to savor and acknowledge it all, a reminder that our connection to nature and the earth extends beyond our understanding.

I often think about the way food colors can impact my emotions. Colors add visual appeal to meals (which encourages us to eat a greater variety of foods) and also influence our mood and behavior. They possess the remarkable ability to stir our emotions and affect our well-being. Picture the allure of a radiant red tomato, an ode to freshness and vitality. Then there's the jeweled green spinach, an invitation to health and vibrancy. A mountain of sunny yellow lemons, a bursting sign of happiness. The colorful produce are the painters of our moods.

Next time you're at the grocery store, pause for a few seconds to reflect on how a colorful vegetable or fruit makes you feel. Allow those emotions to guide your meal plan.

Raita

MAKES 3 CUPS

1 cup plain plant-based yogurt

2 cups shredded English cucumber (1 cucumber)

Juice of 1 lemon (about 2 tablespoons)

Kosher salt

Like Greek tzatziki, raita is made with yogurt and cucumbers. Cool and refreshing, a large dollop of raita is paired with most Indian dishes to help balance out spicines.

Place the yogurt and cucumber in a medium bowl and stir them together. Stir in the lemon juice and season with salt to taste. Serve immediately. If you wish, you can mix together the yogurt and cucumber a day in advance. But to avoid waterlogging the sauce, don't add the lemon juice and salt until you're ready to serve.

Pakora Pancakes

SERVES 4

2 tablespoons neutral oil

4 cups shredded vegetables, such as carrots, kale, thinly sliced onions, and cabbage

½ teaspoon ground cumin

½ teaspoon black salt (kala namak) (optional)

¼ teaspoon ground turmeric

¼ teaspoon ground cayenne

½ cup chickpea flour

½ teaspoon baking soda

2 tablespoons plain plant-based yogurt

2 garlic cloves, grated

1-inch knob fresh ginger, grated (about 1 teaspoon)

1 Thai chili, chopped

Juice of ½ lime (about 1 tablespoon)

1½ teaspoons kosher salt

Chopped scallions or fresh herbs, for garnish

Cilantro Chutney (page 4), for serving

Pakoras, vegetable fritters that are commonly served with tea in India and Pakistan, are an all-day food for me. My riff turns pakoras into spiced pancakes that are made with gluten-free chickpea flour (also known as gram or garbanzo flour, or besan). To make them healthier, instead of frying, I cook the pancakes in a nonstick skillet and serve them for breakfast, lunch, or dinner.

1. Heat 1 tablespoon of the oil in a large nonstick skillet over medium heat. Add the vegetables and stir in the ground cumin, black salt (if using), turmeric, and cayenne. Cook, stirring occasionally, until the vegetables are slightly cooked and any greens are wilted, about 5 minutes. Transfer to a large bowl and let the mixture cool. Drain any excess liquid. Set aside.

2. In a separate large bowl, combine the chickpea flour, baking soda, yogurt, garlic, ginger, Thai chili, lime juice, and salt. Add ⅓ cup plus 1 tablespoon water and whisk until smooth. Add the vegetables to the batter and stir to combine.

3. Wipe out the skillet and heat the remaining 1 tablespoon oil over medium heat. Ladle ¼ cup of the vegetable batter into the skillet and spread it into an even layer. Ladle additional batter into the skillet or work in batches if needed. Reduce the heat to low and cook, covered, until the edges of the pancakes are set, 3 to 5 minutes. Flip and cook them on the other side, another 3 to 5 minutes. Garnish the pancakes with scallions and serve with chutney alongside.

Grilled Pineapple & Peppers with Salsa

SERVES 4

Salsa

1 cup finely chopped fresh parsley leaves

½ cup finely chopped fresh cilantro leaves

2 tablespoons finely chopped fresh mint

2 garlic cloves, minced

½ cup olive oil

2 tablespoons apple cider vinegar

2 teaspoons amchur (mango powder)

1 teaspoon ground cumin

¼ teaspoon crushed red pepper flakes

Kosher salt and freshly ground black pepper

Pineapple & Peppers

2 yellow, orange, or red bell peppers

2 tablespoons neutral oil

3 tablespoons chaat masala

1 ripe pineapple

Pineapple and sweet peppers are a dynamite combo for grilling. Both are high in sugar and caramelize over the high heat from a gas or charcoal grill. Because the flesh of a pineapple is nice and firm, it won't break apart while you're grilling it. Adding chaat masala and herbs makes this a summer staple side dish. These grilled pineapple rounds and sweet peppers are a make-ahead recipe.

1. **Make the salsa:** In a medium bowl, whisk together all the salsa ingredients. Taste and adjust the seasoning as desired. Transfer the salsa to a small bowl and let it sit for at least 30 minutes to allow the flavors to meld together.

2. **Make the pineapple and peppers:** Preheat the grill to medium-high heat.

3. Rub the peppers with 1 tablespoon of the oil and grill until charred on all sides. Transfer to a small bowl, cover with a plate, and let sit for 10 minutes. Peel the darker charred skin off the peppers and discard. Scrape out the seeds and cut the peppers into strips. Sprinkle with 1 tablespoon of the chaat masala and set aside.

4. Trim the top and bottom off the pineapple and slice off the outer skin. Cut the pineapple into slices about ½ inch thick. Brush with the remaining 1 tablespoon oil and sprinkle both sides of each slice with the remaining 2 tablespoons chaat masala. Grill the slices until grill marks appear and the pineapple is heated through, 3 to 4 minutes on each side.

5. Serve the grilled pineapple topped with the bell peppers and drizzle the salsa on top.

Summer Peach & Corn Salad

SERVES 4

¼ cup olive oil

Juice of 1 lime (about 2 tablespoons)

2 teaspoons ground cumin

½ teaspoon Kashmiri chili powder or paprika

Kosher salt and freshly ground black pepper

4 ears corn, shucked

2 fresh peaches, pitted and thinly sliced

1 serrano chili, thinly sliced

¼ cup chopped fresh cilantro

½ cup torn fresh basil

1 small red onion, thinly sliced

Succulent Georgia peaches and fire-roasted corn are what make this the summer "it salad." As the days get warmer and grilling becomes a weeknight occasion, I find myself buying fresh bushels of corn and boxes of Georgia-grown peaches. My Indian ingredients and Georgia peaches are the perfect duo. Buy fresh, young corn at the peak of the season with tight, hydrated green husks and golden-colored corn silk (not dark brown).

1. Preheat the grill to 450°F.

2. Whisk together the olive oil, lime juice, cumin, Kashmiri chili powder, and salt and black pepper to taste in a large bowl. Set aside.

3. Place the corn on the grill over direct heat, cover, and cook for 5 minutes. Rotate each ear a quarter turn, cover, and continue to cook for 5 more minutes. Repeat on all sides of the corn, 15 to 20 minutes total. The corn should have charred spots when cooked through. Remove from the heat.

4. Stand each ear of corn on its end on a cutting board and slice the kernels off the cob, adding them to the dressing as you go, while the kernels are still hot. Cool for 10 minutes.

5. Add the peaches, serrano chili slices, cilantro, basil, and red onion to the corn just before serving and mix well.

Plum & Cherry Salad

SERVES 4

2 tablespoons olive oil

¼ cup fresh orange juice (from 2 medium oranges)

2 tablespoons pure maple syrup

1 teaspoon ground fennel

¼ teaspoon ground cardamom

¼ teaspoon black salt (kala namak)

Freshly ground black pepper

1½ cups Greek-style vanilla plant-based yogurt

4 ripe plums, pitted and sliced into wedges

1 cup cherries, pitted and sliced in half

¼ cup toasted pumpkin seeds

1 tablespoon chopped fresh dill

Fresh plums and cherries are the epitome of juicy sweetness in a summer salad. Their dark, moody hues provide a stark contrast to the vanilla yogurt underneath, creating a dazzling dish. The salad builds to a delicious crescendo with the addition of an orange spiced vinaigrette.

1. In a small bowl, whisk together the olive oil, orange juice, maple syrup, fennel, cardamom, and black salt. Season with pepper to taste.

2. To assemble the salad, spread the yogurt on a serving plate and arrange the plums and cherries on top. Drizzle with the dressing. Sprinkle with the pumpkin seeds and dill.

Coconut Green Beans

SERVES 4 TO 6

1 pound green beans

¼ cup unsweetened coconut
flakes

2 teaspoons neutral oil

½ teaspoon black
mustard seeds

Kosher salt

¼ teaspoon ground turmeric

¼ teaspoon ground cayenne

⅛ teaspoon asafoetida (hing)

1 teaspoon fresh lemon juice

1 teaspoon freshly grated
lemon zest

NOTES

• *Crushed red
pepper flakes can
be substituted for
cayenne.*

• *Almond flour may
be substituted for
coconut flakes.*

• *If you want to scale
up the recipe, use
a food processor to
coarsely pulse the
green beans.*

These coconut green beans are a terrific Thanksgiving substitute for the old-fashioned green bean casserole. Bright and lemony, the dish helps balance the richness of the holiday's heavier sides. Of course, you don't have to wait for Thanksgiving to make this. I serve it as a vegetable side with dal and rice; it cooks quickly with no blanching required. Haricots verts are thinner and more tender than regular green beans. If substituted, they'll cook a little faster.

1. Trim the ends of the green beans, then cut the beans into ¼-inch-long pieces.

2. Heat a large dry skillet over medium-low heat. Add the coconut flakes and cook, stirring constantly, until they smell nutty and turn light brown, 3 to 5 minutes. Transfer to a small bowl and set aside.

3. Wipe the skillet with a clean kitchen towel, add the oil, and heat over medium heat until the oil is shimmering. Add the mustard seeds and cook until they sputter, about 1 minute. Add the green beans, ½ teaspoon salt, the turmeric, cayenne, and asafoetida. Drizzle with the lemon juice and stir to combine. Cook, stirring frequently, until the green beans are slightly cooked but still retain their vibrant green color and crunch, about 5 minutes. If using haricots verts, reduce the cooking time to 3 minutes.

4. Sprinkle the green beans with half of the coconut flakes, the lemon zest, and ½ teaspoon salt. Stir to combine and cook for about 1 minute more. Taste and adjust the seasoning as desired. Remove from the heat and garnish with the remaining coconut. Serve immediately.

Roasted Beets & Greens

6 medium red and golden beets with their leafy tops

3 tablespoons olive oil

2 tablespoons whole grain spicy mustard

Juice of ½ lemon (about 1 tablespoon)

2 teaspoons pure maple syrup

Kosher salt and freshly ground black pepper

½ teaspoon black mustard seeds

¼ teaspoon ground turmeric

This red and golden roasted beet salad uses both the earthy beets and the green tops. Nothing is wasted. Roasting the beets intensifies their flavors while adding a caramelized touch. Although the beets can be roasted and dressed ahead of time and refrigerated until ready to use, the greens should be sautéed right before serving for freshness. This can be served as an appetizer or side dish.

1. Preheat the oven to 400°F.

2. Trim the beet greens, leaving about an inch of stems intact. Wash the beets and greens thoroughly to remove any dirt and pat them dry.

3. Place each beet on a separate square of aluminum foil. Wrap the beets tightly in the foil, creating individual packets. Arrange the foil packets on a large baking sheet and place them in the oven. Roast for about 45 minutes, until tender when pierced with a fork. (Cooking times vary based on the beets' size.)

4. While the beets are roasting, remove any tough stems from the beet greens and discard. Cut the beet greens into bite-size pieces. Set aside.

5. In a large bowl, whisk together 2 tablespoons of the olive oil, the spicy mustard, lemon juice, and maple syrup until well combined. Season with salt and pepper to taste. Set aside.

6. Once the beets are cool enough to handle, gently peel off their skins using your hands or a knife. Slice the beets into wedges and place in the bowl with the dressing. Toss the beets to coat evenly.

7. Heat the remaining 1 tablespoon olive oil in a large sauté pan over medium-high heat until it is shimmering. Add the mustard seeds and cook until they sputter, about 1 minute. Stir in the beet greens and turmeric in batches. Cook until all the greens are wilted but still green, 2 to 3 minutes. Season with salt and pepper to taste and serve.

Vegetable Biryani

SERVES 6 TO 8

1½ cups basmati rice

Kosher salt

¼ teaspoon saffron threads (optional)

½ cup neutral oil

1 large yellow onion, thinly sliced

One 1½-inch cinnamon stick

3 green cardamom pods

1 bay leaf

2 large garlic cloves, minced

1½-inch knob fresh ginger, grated (about 1½ teaspoons)

2 medium Yukon Gold potatoes, peeled and cut into ½-inch cubes (about 2 cups)

2 cups cauliflower cut into bite-size pieces

2 medium carrots, cut into ½-inch pieces

½ cup green beans cut into 2-inch pieces

½ cup plain plant-based yogurt

3 tablespoons Biryani Masala (page xxiv)

½ teaspoon ground turmeric

½ cup fresh mint leaves, plus more for garnish

Raita (page 116), for serving

Biryani is one of the most recognized rice dishes in India, and it delivers a royal effect that's splendidly displayed in front of guests. It's like an Indian paella, a layered dish that's made with basmati rice, marinated vegetables, and optional meat, then mixed with fried onions and freshly ground biryani masala. No other rice compares in taste, appearance, or smell.

Aged basmati has a monopoly on this dish because the grains separate easily, which allows the other ingredients to mix with them to create a uniform dish. Basmati rice lengthens more than other varieties, giving this dish its signature visual appeal of long grains of fluffy rice. There is a crucial step of undercooking the basmati rice so that the grains will soak up the gravy and spices.

1. Place the rice in a large bowl and add cold water to cover. Gently stir the rice with your hands to remove the starch. Drain the rice, return it to the bowl, refill with cold water, and stir again. Repeat the process once more, or until the water runs clear. (Alternatively, you can rinse the rice in a fine-mesh strainer under running water in the sink until the water runs clear.) Add 4 cups fresh water to the bowl. Soak the rice for 30 minutes, then drain.

2. In a large pot, bring 8 cups water with 2 tablespoons salt to a boil over high heat. Add the soaked rice and bring back to a boil, then reduce the heat to medium-high and cook the rice for about 5 minutes. It will be just partially cooked and will have a slight bite in the center. Drain the rice and set aside.

3. Place the saffron threads, if using, in a small bowl with 3 tablespoons warm water. Set aside.

(recipe continues)

4. In a Dutch oven or large heavy-bottomed pan with a lid, heat the oil over medium heat. Add the onion and fry gently until golden brown, stirring occasionally, about 10 minutes. Be careful not to brown it too quickly. Transfer the onion to a plate lined with paper towels to drain. Season with ¼ teaspoon salt immediately and set aside.

5. Add the cinnamon stick, cardamom pods, and bay leaf to the pot with the remaining oil and cook for a minute. Stir in the garlic, ginger, potatoes, cauliflower, carrots, green beans, yogurt, biryani masala, turmeric, and ¼ cup water. Season with salt to taste, cover, and cook for 10 to 12 minutes. The vegetables will be partially cooked.

6. Transfer half of the vegetable mixture to a medium bowl. Layer half of the rice over the vegetable mixture that remains in the Dutch oven. Sprinkle half of the mint leaves and half of the fried onions on top. Layer the rest of the vegetable mixture on top, followed by the remaining rice, mint leaves, and fried onions. Pour the saffron water over the top. Cover the Dutch oven with foil, then cover with the lid to help trap more steam as the biryani cooks. Cook over low heat for 20 to 25 minutes, until the veggies are cooked through and the rice is tender. Garnish with fresh mint leaves and serve hot with raita alongside.

Watermelon Cooler (Sharbat)

SERVES 4 TO 6

8 cups chopped seedless watermelon

Juice of 2 limes (about 4 tablespoons)

1 teaspoon black salt (kala namak)

2 tablespoons rose water

¼ cup pure maple syrup

Ice

Dried rose petals, for garnish (optional)

West India in the summer: the train stations are lined with vendors selling sharbat, India's soft drink. ("Sharbat" is a Persian word that simply refers to a drink made of sugar and water.) My parents would offer chilled sharbat to their guests instead of fizzy drinks or water. The watermelon in this sharbat recipe makes a hydrating drink that's great for quenching thirst on hot summer days.

Place the watermelon, lime juice, black salt, rose water, and maple syrup in a high-speed blender and blend until smooth. Fill serving glasses with ice and pour the sharbat over the ice. Top with dried rose petals, if using, and serve immediately.

Coriander South Side

MAKES 4 COCKTAILS

½ cup Coriander Simple
  Syrup (recipe follows)

8 to 12 mint leaves, plus
  4 sprigs for garnish

8 cucumber slices

1 cup gin, preferably Jin Jiji
  Darjeeling Gin

¼ cup plus 2 tablespoons
  fresh lime juice (from about
  5 limes)

Ice

8 ounces soda water

There is so much to appreciate about this gin cocktail. A complex botanical spirit, gin is a surprisingly good match for coriander seeds. The clean, refreshing taste from the combination of gin, cucumber, lime, and mint can't help but make you feel good, and wait till you see your friends' adoring reactions when they take their first sip of this lively cocktail.

Pour the simple syrup into a shaker and muddle the mint leaves and 4 slices of the cucumber into the syrup. Add the gin and lime juice and fill the shaker with ice. Shake vigorously. Fill four Collins glasses with ice, then strain the gin mixture over the ice. Top each glass with the soda water and garnish with a mint sprig and the remaining cucumber slices.

Coriander Simple Syrup

MAKES 4 CUPS

1 cup coriander seeds

2 cups cane sugar

In a medium saucepan, toast the coriander seeds over medium-low heat until fragrant, about 5 minutes. Add the sugar and 2 cups water. Bring to a boil, then lower to a simmer and cook, stirring, until the sugar has dissolved. Remove from the heat and let cool for 2 hours. Strain the syrup through a fine-mesh strainer into airtight glass jars. Discard the coriander seeds. Store the simple syrup in the refrigerator for up to 1 month.

Food Is
SURPRISING

What can you cook that you couldn't a year ago?

Learning new ways to cook is an art that can be both challenging and rewarding. As we explore new ingredients and techniques, we expand our culinary horizons and open ourselves up to a world of new possibilities. And the best part? With practice, what was once intimidating or unfamiliar can become second nature.

Whether it's mastering a new cooking method, experimenting with an exotic spice, or learning to cook a new cuisine, there are countless ways to expand your cooking skills. And the more you learn, the more confident and creative you'll become in the kitchen.

So what can you make now that you couldn't a year ago? Maybe you've finally mastered a pasta from scratch, or you've learned to cook a new cuisine that rivals your favorite take-out spot. Perhaps you've discovered the novelty of sous vide cooking or the versatility of fermented foods.

Whatever it is, take pride in the fact that you're constantly learning and growing as a cook. And don't be afraid to keep pushing yourself out of your comfort zone and trying new things.

Scrappy Indian Bouillon Cubes

Throughout the photo shoot for this cookbook, I challenged the team to be zero waste with ingredients from the recipes, and I introduced them to my scrappy Indian-inspired bouillon cubes. We saved scraps, peels, and bits of herbs and fruit to make them. Traditional vegetable broths don't have much fiber, but this alternative is chock-full of it. Save all your vegetable and fruit scraps in a bag or airtight container, puree them on a regular basis, season them, and portion them into ice cube trays. When ready to use, melt the cubes in water or broth (2 cubes = 1 cup broth) or sauté them in oil for a flavorful fiber-packed base for soup, stews, or beans. The best part is, you can modify this recipe with other spices and herbs for use in a variety of culinary dishes.

Puree vegetable, herb, and/or fruit scraps in a high-speed blender until smooth. Season to taste with ground cumin, ground coriander, ground turmeric, and salt. Spoon the puree into ice cube trays and freeze until solid. Transfer the cubes to a freezer bag and store in the freezer for up to 3 months.

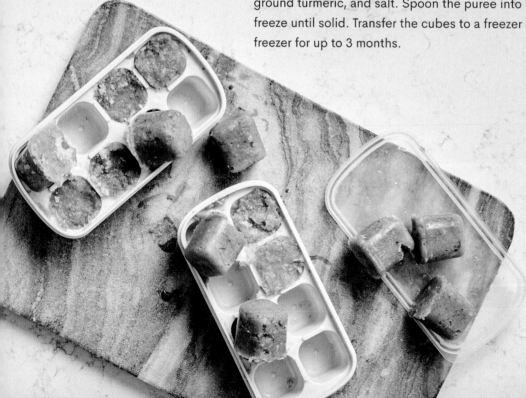

Roasted Mushroom Vindaloo Wraps

SERVES 4

1 pound cremini mushrooms, quartered

2 tablespoons white vinegar

1 tablespoon neutral oil

2-inch knob fresh ginger, chopped (about 1 tablespoon)

3 garlic cloves, grated

2 teaspoons Kashmiri chili powder

1 tablespoon paprika

1 tablespoon ground cumin

1 tablespoon Garam Masala (page xxiii) or store-bought

Kosher salt

Freshly ground black pepper

Raita (page 116) or plain plant-based yogurt

4 Garlic Naan (page 63) or store-bought

1 cup arugula or other salad greens

½ cup sliced cherry tomatoes and/or cucumbers, for garnish (optional)

Vindaloo can be traced back to the Portuguese arriving in Goa; they added vinegar, pepper, garlic, and wine to preserve foods. This dish was adapted by the local community by adding spices such as black pepper, cinnamon, cardamom, cloves, and the key ingredient, which gave bite to the grainy sauce of vindaloo—red chilies. (Interestingly, the Portuguese were also responsible for introducing chilies to India—a fact that's shocking, even for Indians.) Vindaloo spices work with any meaty mushroom variety. In the summer, you can grill the mushrooms for a smokier finish.

1. Preheat the oven to 400°F. Line a 9 × 13-inch baking dish or a rimmed baking sheet with aluminum foil.

2. Place the mushrooms in a large bowl. Add the vinegar, oil, ginger, garlic, spices, 2 teaspoons salt, and ¼ teaspoon black pepper and toss to coat.

3. Spread the mushrooms in a single layer in the lined baking dish. Roast the mushrooms until soft and puckered, about 20 minutes.

4. Remove the mushrooms from the oven and give a good stir to coat with their sauce. Taste and adjust the seasoning, adding more salt and black pepper if needed.

5. Spread the raita on the naan and top with the mushrooms and arugula. Garnish with tomatoes and/or cucumbers, if desired.

Peanut-Avocado Chaat Salad

SERVES 2 TO 4

2 cups salted roasted peanuts

½ cup diced cherry tomatoes

1 avocado, pitted, peeled, and diced

1 small red onion, minced

1 serrano chili, minced (remove seeds for less heat)

1 teaspoon chaat masala

1 teaspoon ground cumin

¼ cup chopped fresh cilantro

Juice of 1 lime (about 2 tablespoons)

Kosher salt

2 tablespoons pomegranate seeds, for garnish (optional)

1 tablespoon chopped fresh mint, for garnish (optional)

Chaat is a style of street food known best for its symphony of crispy, tangy, sweet, and spicy elements that are both warming and cooling. The base recipe for chaat typically consists of cooked items like samosas or unlikely ingredients like avocados or raw mangoes. These serve as a canvas for the myriad fresh toppings and condiments that are added, including tamarind, mint, and cilantro, spread over the crispy base. This quick peanut chaat is so easy to make—it's like a chaat chopped salad.

In a large bowl, mix the peanuts, tomatoes, avocado, onion, serrano chili, chaat masala, cumin, cilantro, and lime juice. Season with salt to taste and let sit for 10 minutes so the flavors meld. If desired, garnish with pomegranate seeds and mint before serving.

Open-Face Chili Cheese Toast

SERVES 2

2 tablespoons plant-based mayonnaise

2 tablespoons finely chopped fresh cilantro

½ cup plant-based shredded cheese, such as Violife or Follow Your Heart

½ red or green bell pepper, cored, seeded, and finely diced

2 Thai chilies, finely minced

¼ teaspoon kosher salt

4 slices multigrain bread

1 large garlic clove, peeled and lightly smashed

Indian Ketchup (Kasundi) (page 37), for serving

Roll call for anyone who likes cheese and chili, and can make toast! This Mumbai bar snack is an open-face grilled cheese sandwich with chilies and bell peppers. Cut into triangles and enjoy as an afternoon snack.

1. Adjust an oven rack closest to the top position and preheat the broiler to high.

2. In a small bowl, stir together the mayonnaise, cilantro, cheese, bell pepper, Thai chilies, and salt.

3. Toast the bread on the lowest toaster setting. Alternatively, you can toast the bread on the stovetop. Heat a large cast-iron or oven-safe pan over medium heat. Toast the bread slices on both sides for 2 minutes, or until the surface is crispy enough to hold the filling.

4. Rub the garlic clove on one side of each toast. Spread the cheese mixture evenly on the bread and place in the warm pan. Place the pan under the broiler until the cheese is melted, 3 to 5 minutes. Cut into triangles and serve hot with Indian ketchup.

Cereal Chex Mix (Chevdo)

MAKES 8 CUPS

¼ cup neutral oil

2 teaspoons black mustard seeds

1 cup raw peanuts

½ cup golden raisins

10 curry leaves

1 tablespoon cane sugar

1 teaspoon ground turmeric

¼ teaspoon Kashmiri chili powder or ground cayenne

⅛ teaspoon asafoetida (hing)

½ tablespoon kosher salt

8 cups cereal mix, such as rice puffs, corn flakes, and wheat flakes

NOTE: *Make sure all ingredients are measured out before cooking the mix, as the spices can quickly burn in the oil.*

Chevdo is a popular snack during the monsoon season in India. The exact origins of chevdo or, as I like to describe it, "Indian Chex mix" are unknown, but the name is derived from the Gujarati word "chevdi," which means "mixture." This is a fitting name for the snack, as it is a delicious blend of different flavors and textures. Chevdo is typically made with a variety of common cereals, such as puffed rice, rice flakes, corn flakes, and wheat flakes. Add-ins include peanuts, dried lentils, spices, and curry leaves. All the ingredients are seasoned with a blend of spices like turmeric and chili powder. Chevdo can be made ahead of time for parties.

1. Heat the oil in a large heavy-bottomed saucepan or wok over medium heat until it is shimmering. Add the mustard seeds and cook until they sputter, about 1 minute. Stir in the peanuts and golden raisins and cook for another 2 minutes. Carefully add the curry leaves (they will sputter) and cook for 30 seconds, or until the sputtering stops. Reduce the heat to low and add the sugar, turmeric, Kashmiri chili powder, asafoetida, and salt to the oil and mix well for 30 seconds.

2. Add the cereal mix and toss until well coated. Cook for 1 to 2 minutes. Taste and adjust the seasoning as needed. Remove from the heat and cool completely. Store the chevdo in an airtight container in a cool, dry place for up to 2 weeks.

Leek & Potato Chickpea Frittata

SERVES 4 TO 6

1¼ cups chickpea flour

½ serrano chili, chopped

1 garlic clove, minced

1 tablespoon nutritional yeast

1½ teaspoons Garam Masala (page xxiii) or store-bought

1 teaspoon ground turmeric

¼ teaspoon ground cayenne

¼ teaspoon black salt (kala namak)

¼ teaspoon freshly ground black pepper

Juice of ½ lemon (about 1 tablespoon)

2 cups frozen shredded hash brown potatoes, thawed

3 tablespoons neutral oil

1 leek, halved lengthwise, rinsed well, white and light green parts thinly sliced (about 2 cups)

4 scallions, white and light green parts, chopped

1 large orange bell pepper, cored, seeded, and chopped

1½ teaspoons kosher salt

New York brunch is legendary, and I have many fond memories of relaxing and unwinding with friends over leisurely weekend brunches. The conviviality of a one-pan dish like frittata is something I'm a fan of—especially when I'm hosting at home and want to spend less time in the kitchen. This plant-based frittata relies on a medley of brunch staples, like potatoes, peppers, and leeks, that are combined with chickpea flour in place of eggs.

1. Preheat the oven to 400°F.

2. Place the chickpea flour in a large bowl, add 1 cup water, and whisk to remove any lumps. Stir in the serrano chili, garlic, nutritional yeast, garam masala, turmeric, cayenne, black salt, black pepper, and lemon juice. Fold in the hash browns. The batter should coat all the potatoes, without being runny. If the batter is too thick, add water, a tablespoon at a time.

3. Heat the oil in a 10-inch oven-safe skillet or cast-iron pan over medium heat until it is shimmering. Add the leek, three-quarters of the scallions, and the bell pepper and sprinkle with the kosher salt. Sauté to soften the vegetables, 3 to 5 minutes. Increase the heat to medium-high. Scrape the batter into the skillet, using a spatula to flatten and even out the surface. Cover and cook until the edges begin to firm, 8 to 10 minutes. Transfer the skillet to the oven and cook until the center of the frittata has set and the edges are lightly browned, 20 to 25 minutes. Remove from the oven and cool for 10 minutes. Invert the dish to a large serving plate, cut into portions, and serve with a small green salad for each guest. Optional: cut into portions and serve directly from the skillet.

Roasted Butternut Squash with Makhani Sauce

SERVES 4

Butternut Squash

2 teaspoons ground cinnamon

½ teaspoon ground cloves

1 teaspoon Kashmiri chili powder

1 teaspoon ground turmeric

1 large (about 3 pounds) butternut squash, peeled, seeded, and cut into ¼-inch-thick slices

Kosher salt

2 tablespoons neutral oil

Makhani Sauce

2 tablespoons neutral oil

1 medium yellow onion, chopped

3 medium Roma (plum) tomatoes, roughly chopped

2 garlic cloves, minced

1-inch knob fresh ginger, grated (about 1 teaspoon)

2 teaspoons Kashmiri chili powder

½ teaspoon ground turmeric

½ teaspoon Garam Masala (page xxiii) or store-bought

½ cup raw cashews, soaked overnight or microwaved in hot water for 2 minutes and set aside for 20 minutes, rinsed and drained

1 teaspoon cane sugar

Kosher salt

1 tablespoon dried fenugreek leaves (kasoori methi), crushed, plus more for garnish

2 tablespoons pomegranate seeds, for garnish

When makhani or makhan is listed in a dish, it refers to butter or cream. The silky makhani sauce is traditionally made by simmering spices in butter, and it pairs well with fall squashes. For a creamy finish, I use cashews. Note that the cashews must be soaked overnight or microwaved in hot water for 2 minutes and set aside for 20 minutes before preparing the sauce, so plan accordingly.

1. Preheat the oven to 400°F. Line a rimmed baking sheet with a silicone baking mat or aluminum foil.

2. **Make the butternut squash:** Whisk together the cinnamon, cloves, Kashmiri chili powder, and turmeric in a small bowl. Toss the squash with the oil, the salt to taste, and the spice mixture and spread it out over the prepared baking sheet. Roast until tender when pierced with a fork, about 30 minutes, rotating once during cooking.

3. **Make the makhani sauce:** Heat the oil in a large Dutch oven over medium-high heat. Add the onion and cook until golden brown, 5 to 7 minutes. Add the tomatoes, garlic, ginger, Kashmiri chili powder, turmeric, and garam masala. Cook until the tomatoes have softened, about 5 minutes. Transfer the mixture to a high-speed blender, add the cashews and 1 cup water, and puree until creamy. Return the puree to the Dutch oven. Add the sugar, season with salt to taste, and simmer until the gravy until has thickened, 8 to 10 minutes. Stir in the crushed fenugreek leaves. Taste and adjust the seasoning, adding more salt if needed.

4. Spoon the sauce onto a serving plate and arrange the roasted squash slices on top. Garnish with additional fenugreek leaves and pomegranate seeds. Serve immediately.

Almond Cookies with Omani Lime

MAKES 1 DOZEN COOKIES

2 large dried Omani limes

2 cups almond flour

¼ cup all-purpose flour

1 teaspoon baking soda

¼ teaspoon kosher salt

8 tablespoons (1 stick) plant-based butter, softened

⅓ cup cane sugar

1 teaspoon pure vanilla extract

¼ cup plain oat milk

12 blanched almonds

2 tablespoons powdered sugar

When I first had these cookies, handmade by a chef I met in Oman, trying to figure out what I was tasting was like a pop quiz for my palate. Turns out, his secret was Omani limes—the dried limes usually used for savory cooking. It took me a few years to master taming down the tanginess of the lime to keep it from overpowering the cookie. This recipe strikes the right balance between tart and sweet.

1. Place an oven rack in the middle position and preheat the oven to 350°F. Line a baking sheet with a silicone baking mat or parchment paper.

2. Place the Omani limes in a spice grinder or mortar and pestle to grind into a fine powder. Transfer 1 tablespoon of the powder to a medium bowl, reserving any remaining powder in a small glass jar for another use. Add the almond flour, all-purpose flour, baking soda, and salt to the lime powder, stirring to combine. Set aside.

3. In a separate medium bowl, beat the butter, cane sugar, vanilla, and oat milk with an electric hand mixer on low speed or with a large whisk until well-combined, about 3 minutes. Fold in the dry ingredients and mix until combined.

4. Divide the dough into twelve 1-inch balls and arrange them 2 inches apart on the prepared baking sheet. Gently press 1 almond on top of each ball, flattening the ball slightly to create a flat bottom but still maintaining a mounded shape.

5. Bake, rotating the pan halfway through baking, until the center has set and the cookies are golden brown, about 18 minutes. Let cool on the baking sheet for 10 minutes to firm up. Dust the cookies with the powdered sugar. Store them in an airtight container in a cool, dry place at room temperature for up to 1 week.

Cantaloupe Masala Shaved Ice

SERVES 4

4 cups chopped cantaloupe (from a 1½-pound cantaloupe)

½ cup cane sugar

⅓ cup lime juice (from about 4 limes)

¼ cup fresh mint leaves

½ teaspoon chaat masala

½ teaspoon ground cumin

½ teaspoon freshly ground black pepper

⅛ teaspoon black salt (kala namak)

Mint sprigs, for garnish

Shaved iced (golas) is as loved as ice cream in India for cooling down from the summer heat. The word "gola" comes from the Sanskrit word "golaka," which means "ball." A giant block of ice is chiseled by hand, then the ice is shaved in a wooden machine into fluffy clouds that are shaped into a cone. Vendors crowd streets in the summer with an array of colored syrups neatly lined up on their wooden carts. This cantaloupe shaved ice recipe takes me back to slurping down golas as a kid.

1. Place all the ingredients except the mint garnish in a high-speed blender, add ¼ cup water, and puree until smooth, 1 to 2 minutes. Strain through a fine-mesh sieve into a shallow 9 × 13-inch glass baking dish. Discard the solids. Place the cantaloupe mixture in the freezer. After 1 hour, scrape the surface of the mixture with a fork, working from the edges into the middle. Freeze again.

2. Repeat the scraping four more times, every 30 to 45 minutes, breaking up large chunks with a fork until the mixture is fully frozen and looks like shaved ice, about a total of 3 hours.

3. To serve, scape and divide the shaved ice into cups and garnish each with a sprig of fresh mint.

NOTES

• The shaved ice can be prepared up to 2 days ahead. Wrap the baking dish in plastic wrap.

• You can substitute other melon varieties.

Spiced Phyllo Cake

Syrup

1 cup cane sugar

3 strips orange zest

½ cup fresh orange juice
(from 2 oranges)

One 1½-inch cinnamon stick

2 star anise

4 cloves

3 green cardamom pods,
lightly smashed

Cake

16 ounces phyllo dough,
thawed

Cooking spray

1 cup aquafaba (see
page xxvii)

¾ cup cane sugar

1 cup plain plant-based
yogurt

¾ cup neutral oil

1 tablespoon grated
orange zest

½ cup fresh orange juice
(from 2 oranges)

1 tablespoon cornstarch

1 teaspoon pure vanilla
extract

2 teaspoons baking powder

Dried orange slices, for
garnish (optional)

I had the most unforgettable dessert in Saudi Arabia—a traditional Greek cake with oranges. The memory of that cake has stayed with me over time, compelling me to create my own version using warming spices like star anise, cloves, and cinnamon, spices that are always at the ready in my pantry. I'm always learning to showcase Indian spices in new ways.

1. Preheat the oven to 300°F.

2. Make the syrup: Combine the sugar, ½ cup water, the orange zest, orange juice, and spices in a small saucepan and bring to a boil over medium-high heat. Let simmer, stirring occasionally, until the sugar has dissolved and the syrup has thickened, about 10 minutes. Strain into a small bowl and set aside to cool while you make the cake.

3. Make the cake: To dry the phyllo dough, remove the thawed phyllo from the package and unfold each roll. Carefully take a single sheet from one roll and lay it flat on a large baking sheet. With your fingertips on the bottom short edge of the sheet, pleat the sheet like an accordion (without intricate folding). Repeat with the remaining sheets from this roll and then repeat the process, gathering the sheets from the second phyllo roll on a second large baking sheet. Bake to dry the phyllo so it's crisp but not browned, 15 to 20 minutes. Let cool completely and then use your hands to crush the dried phyllo into small pieces, like confetti.

(recipe continues)

NOTES

• *Phyllo dough can be separated onto baking sheets and left inside an oven overnight to dry.*

• *If you don't have a springform cake pan, use a 9 × 3-inch baking dish.*

4. Increase the oven temperature to 350°F.

5. Lightly coat a 9 × 3-inch round springform cake pan with cooking spray, line the bottom with parchment, then spray the parchment. Set the pan on a large baking sheet.

6. In a large bowl, whisk together the aquafaba, sugar, yogurt, oil, zest, orange juice, cornstarch, and vanilla. Add the baking powder and lightly whisk to incorporate.

7. Add the phyllo pieces and gently fold them into the batter until moistened. Scrape the phyllo batter into the prepared springform pan and spread it out evenly. Bake until golden and a toothpick inserted at the center of the cake comes out clean, about 45 minutes.

8. While the cake is still hot, use a paring knife to pierce small holes all over it. Pour the cooled syrup over the hot cake, distributing it evenly over the whole surface. Run a knife around the inside edge of the pan to loosen the cake and then unmold it from the pan. Garnish with the dried orange slices, if using.

Meyer Lemon Meringue Pie

Crust

1⅓ cups all-purpose flour, plus more for the work surface

1 tablespoon cane sugar

¼ teaspoon kosher salt

8 tablespoons (1 stick) plant-based butter, cold, cut into small pieces

1 teaspoon white vinegar

Filling

1½ cups plain soy or oat milk (or any plant-based milk), preferably a barista blend

1 cup cane sugar

Grated zest of 2 Meyer lemons

½ cup Meyer lemon juice (from about 6 lemons; see Notes on page 159)

¼ cup plus 2 tablespoons cornstarch

Scant pinch of saffron threads (see Notes on page 159)

Meringue Topping

½ cup reduced aquafaba (from ¾ cup before reducing; see page xxvii)

½ teaspoon cream of tartar

Pinch of kosher salt

½ cup cane sugar

1 teaspoon lemon zest

½ teaspoon pure vanilla extract

This is a statement pie, with Meyer lemons, fluffy, cloud-like meringue piled high, and hints of saffron. It's also a statement of how far plant-based baking has come. To the person who discovered the magic of chickpea cooking liquid (aquafaba), I'm grateful—when concentrated to a viscous consistency, it whips like egg whites. Who knew that something typically poured down the drain could transform baking forever? You can opt for a vegan store-bought pie crust if you wish and still beam with pride at this glorious pie.

1. Make the crust: In the bowl of a food processor (or in a stand mixer or using your fingers), work quickly to incorporate the flour, sugar, salt, and butter. Pulse three to five times (or mix by hand) until the mixture is uniform and resembles coarse cornmeal. Transfer the flour–butter mixture to a large bowl.

2. In a small bowl, mix the vinegar with 4 tablespoons cold water. Stir it into the flour mixture and press the dough together. If it's too crumbly, add more water, 1 tablespoon at a time, to bring the dough together without overworking it. Turn the dough out onto a lightly floured work surface and gently knead it together, combining parts of the mixture that are wetter with those that are drier.

3. Form the dough into a disc and wrap it with plastic wrap. Refrigerate for 1 hour (or up to 2 days); bring to room temperature for 10 minutes before rolling it out. Roll out the dough on a lightly floured surface into an even circle, about 13 inches in diameter and ⅛ inch thick.

4. Fold the dough in half, or roll it loosely around the rolling pin, and gently lift and position it over a 9-inch pie plate. Unfold or unroll the dough, fitting it into the pie plate. Press the dough gently against the sides and bottom. Trim the overhang to ½ inch. Flute the dough edges

(recipe continues)

• You can replace the saffron with a scant pinch of ground turmeric.

• If you cannot find Meyer lemons, replace the 6 needed in this recipe for 4 regular lemons.

by pressing a finger against the inside edge of the pastry and into the index finger of the other hand, or crimp the outer edges with a fork. Loosely cover with foil and refrigerate or freeze for about 30 minutes.

5. Preheat the oven to 425°F.

6. Line the pie crust with aluminum foil and fill with pie weights (tip: sugar or rice make great pie weights). The foil will keep the walls of the pie crust from sliding down while under heat. Bake until deep golden brown, 12 to 14 minutes. Transfer to a cooling rack and remove the foil and pie weights. Let the crust cool completely.

7. Make the filling: Whisk together the soy milk, sugar, lemon zest, lemon juice, cornstarch, and saffron in a medium heavy-bottomed saucepan over medium-low heat, eliminating any lumps. Cook, continuing to whisk, until the sugar has dissolved and the custard begins to bubble and thicken, 3 to 5 minutes. Pour the lemon custard into the cooled pie crust. Place a piece of plastic wrap on the surface of the custard to prevent a skin from forming and refrigerate until firm, 4 to 6 hours.

8. Make the meringue topping: Preheat the oven to 350°F. (Skip preheating the oven if you would instead prefer to use a blowtorch to brown the meringue.)

9. Place the aquafaba, cream of tartar, and salt in a medium bowl. Use an electric hand mixer fitted with the whisk attachment to whisk together on medium speed until lightly frothy, about 2 minutes. Mix in ¼ cup of the sugar, a little at a time. Mix in the lemon zest and vanilla. Add the remaining ¼ cup sugar, then increase the mixer speed to high. Mix until the meringue holds stiff peaks, about 5 minutes.

10. Using a rubber spatula, scoop the meringue on top of the pie. Use the spatula or the back of a spoon to create swirls.

11. Bake the pie until the meringue is golden brown around the peaks, 10 to 12 minutes. (Alternatively, use a blowtorch: starting about 6 inches from the pie, move the torch over the meringue in a circular motion until the meringue is golden brown and caramelized, about 5 minutes.)

Food Is
INVITING

What is your most treasured tradition when hosting?

Traditions are timeless threads that weave our story. They are a melody that resonates through generations, connecting us to each other.

Over the generations, my family has kept a heartfelt tradition when hosting milestone events: gifting each guest an engraved piece of stainless steel kitchenware. In India, this practice involves etching a family's name and other significant details onto the steel to commemorate special moments. Engraved kitchenware is given out to friends and family for various occasions, such as weddings and births, or even in times of mourning. My mom has her own heirloom piece, handed down from her mother, and these culinary heirlooms continue to be passed down through the generations. The act of engraving holds a special place in my heart. I fondly remember watching my grandmother cook with her cherished kitchenware, and even when I washed them, I would run my fingers over the engraved letters.

When I host, my goal is to create an inviting space where people can come together, share their stories, and forge new connections. My tradition is to add a touch of intrigue by placing conversation prompt cards under each plate, encouraging guests to engage and connect with one another. For me, this is an opportunity to channel my creativity through food, decor, and ambiance, bringing people together in a way that is both profound and memorable: The guests share experiences, moments of vulnerability, and heartfelt conversations that linger in their memories long after the dinner.

As I reflect on my past gatherings, I can't help but smile, recalling the infectious laughter, the animated chatter, and the melodious clinking of glasses that have reverberated through every corner of my house.

Dash & Chutney Hot Sauce

MAKES ½ CUP

6 serrano chilies

1 teaspoon neutral oil

1 cup chopped fresh cilantro

¼ cup fresh mint leaves

¼ cup plant-based
    mayonnaise

Juice from ½ lemon (about
    1 tablespoon)

1 tablespoon white vinegar

1 teaspoon ground coriander

1 teaspoon ground cumin

Kosher salt

This hot sauce, which makes the lips and body tingle, was created for my heat-seeking customers. The charred serrano chilies are balanced with grassy herbs and the fruity notes of lemon and spices.

1. Turn your exhaust fan to high and open the windows! Rinse and dry the chilies thoroughly using a clean kitchen towel, to prevent splattering.

2. Heat a small cast-iron skillet or heavy-bottomed pan over medium-high heat. In a small bowl, toss the serrano chilies with the oil to coat. Cook the chilies in a single layer, turning them every minute or so, until charred all around, 5 to 7 minutes. Transfer them to a small bowl to cool.

3. Place the cooled chilies, cilantro, mint, mayonnaise, lemon juice, vinegar, spices, and 1 teaspoon salt in a high-speed blender. Add 2 tablespoons water and puree until smooth, about 1 minute. Taste and adjust the seasoning as desired.

4. Store the hot sauce in an airtight container in the refrigerator for up to 2 weeks.

Whipped Spiced Butter & Crispy Seeds

MAKES 1 CUP

Whipped Butter

2 sticks unsalted plant-based
  butter, softened

3 tablespoons olive oil

¼ teaspoon pink
  Himalayan salt

Crispy Seeds

2 tablespoons neutral oil

3 tablespoons whole
  cumin seeds

3 tablespoons
  coriander seeds

Kosher salt

I'm a sucker for a good bread basket accompanied by oil or butter. Quality plant-based butter tastes similar to dairy butter, so I've reimagined whipped butter from my culinary school days, replacing it with a vegan option and mixing in crispy sautéed seeds to make a compound butter.

1. Make the whipped butter: Place the softened butter in a small bowl and add the olive oil and salt. Whisk by hand until light and creamy. (Alternatively, use an electric hand mixer: start on low speed to combine and then gradually increase the speed until the oil is fully incorporated into the butter.)

2. Make the crispy seeds: Heat the oil in a medium skillet over medium-low heat. Add the cumin seeds and coriander seeds and sauté until golden brown and aromatic, about 5 minutes. Remove from the pan to a plate to cool. Mix the seeds with the whipped butter, season with salt to taste, and serve. Store in a glass container and refrigerate for up to 3 months.

Multi-Seed Turmeric Crackers

SERVES 4

½ cup raw pumpkin seeds

¼ cup mixed black and white sesame seeds

3 tablespoons chia seeds

½ cup oat flour or almond flour

¼ cup ground flaxseed

1 teaspoon ground turmeric

½ teaspoon kosher salt

¼ teaspoon freshly ground black pepper

2 tablespoons olive oil

NOTES

• *To make oat flour, blend old-fashioned oats, quick oats, or steel-cut oats in a high-speed blender until the oats turn into a fine flour, about 1 minute. Store any extra flour in an airtight container for up to 3 months.*

• *The cracker dough can be made 1 week ahead. Store in an airtight container in the refrigerator.*

These turmeric crackers are gluten-free and easy to modify with any other seeds or nuts. Enjoy them on their own as a crunchy snack, or pair them with Eggplant Dip (Bharta Style) (page 168), hummus, or Garlic-Sesame Chili Oil (page 86). This is an ideal cracker that has it all.

1. Preheat the oven to 300°F.

2. In a large bowl, combine the pumpkin seeds, sesame seeds, chia seeds, flour, ground flaxseed, turmeric, salt, and pepper. Mix well to ensure even distribution of the ingredients.

3. In a small bowl, whisk the olive oil with ½ cup water. Pour the wet mixture into the dry mixture and stir until a dough forms. You may need to use your hands to knead the dough gently to incorporate all the ingredients.

4. Place the dough on a 12 × 16-inch sheet of parchment paper set on a flat surface and cover it with another sheet of parchment paper. (This will prevent the dough from sticking to the rolling pin.) Roll out the dough between the two sheets of parchment paper to about ⅛-inch thickness.

5. Transfer the rolled-out dough onto a baking sheet, then remove the top sheet of parchment. Bake for 40 minutes, or until the edges are golden brown and the crackers are crisp. Keep an eye on it, as baking time may vary depending on the thickness of the dough.

6. Transfer to a wire rack to cool completely. The cracker will continue to crisp up as it cools. Once cooled, break into pieces with your hands.

7. Store the crackers in an airtight container in a cool, dry place for up to 2 weeks.

Eggplant Dip (Bharta Style)

SERVES 4 TO 6

1 medium eggplant (about 1 pound)

1 tablespoon neutral oil

1 small yellow onion, diced

Kosher salt

¼ teaspoon cumin seeds

¼ teaspoon Kashmiri chili powder

¼ teaspoon ground coriander

¼ teaspoon ground turmeric

¼ teaspoon Garam Masala (page xxiii) or store-bought

1 cup cherry tomatoes, halved

1 teaspoon lemon juice

1 tablespoon chopped fresh cilantro, for garnish

Charring eggplant over an open fire brings it to new heights by layering flavors. In my book there's no other way to make eggplant. This method reigns supreme in taste and texture and gives the eggplant an alluring smoky, sultry aroma. I've converted what is typically a side dish into a dip with crackers for a fun new spread for entertaining.

1. Line the top of a gas stove with aluminum foil, leaving the burners and pilot exposed, to collect the dripping juices from the eggplant as it cooks. Place the eggplant directly on the burner over a medium-high flame and cook for 15 to 20 minutes, using tongs to turn it every few minutes for even cooking. The eggplant is done when the skin is charred and the flesh has collapsed and softened.

2. For the oven method, prick the eggplant all over with a fork and rub with oil, then place in a baking dish or on a rimmed baking sheet lined with aluminum foil. Roast at 400°F for 45 to 50 minutes, turning halfway through, until the skin is charred and the flesh has collapsed and softened.

3. Let cool for 10 minutes, then remove the ends and the skin and roughly chop the eggplant.

4. Heat the oil in a sauté pan over medium-high heat. Add the onion and 1 teaspoon salt and cook until the onion is translucent, about 5 minutes. Add the spices and cherry tomatoes and sauté until the tomatoes soften, about another 5 minutes. Stir in the chopped eggplant and lemon juice and season with salt to taste. Cook, covered, over low heat for 3 to 4 minutes.

5. Transfer the eggplant mixture to the bowl of a food chopper and pulse three to five times, until the mixture is combined but slightly chunky. Taste and adjust the seasoning as needed. Transfer to a serving bowl and garnish with cilantro. Serve with Multi-Seed Turmeric Crackers (page 166) or your choice of crackers.

Layered Bread (Lacha Paratha)

MAKES 6 PARATHAS

2 cups white whole wheat flour, plus more for dusting and rolling

1 teaspoon kosher salt

5 tablespoons coconut oil or plant-based butter, melted, plus more for serving

A light, flaky, crispy bread that you rip apart with your fingers to use for lapping up sauce, butter, or chili oil, lacha paratha is made with just a few ingredients, like a flatbread. The signature layers for this paratha require rolling a piece of dough thinner than a regular roti, then brushing it with fat (in this case, coconut oil or vegan butter), coiling it up into a snail shape, and rolling it out again. To make a flavored lacha paratha, add a sprinkling of cumin powder, salt, cilantro, or any other spices on top of the fat that is brushed on the dough.

1. In a large bowl, stir together the flour, salt, and 1 tablespoon of the melted coconut oil until combined. Add ⅔ cup water, mixing to form a sticky dough. Knead the dough, adding water as needed, 1 tablespoon at a time, to make a smooth, soft ball. Cover the bowl with a damp clean kitchen towel and let rest for 30 minutes.

2. On a lightly floured surface, divide the dough into 6 equal pieces. Roll each piece into a 1½-inch ball. Working with 1 dough ball at a time, flatten the dough with your palm, dust with flour, and roll out into a thin 6-inch round.

3. Brush the dough with coconut oil and sprinkle with more flour. Starting at the edge closest to you, fold the dough into thin accordion pleats that stack on each other.

4. Stretch the pleated dough as much as possible into a rope (it may stretch only 1 inch or so), pressing down on the pleats to keep them intact. Spiral the pleated dough around itself like a rose. Pinch the ends of the dough together to secure. Dust the spiral with more flour. Repeat with the remaining balls of dough. Let the coiled parathas rest for 15 minutes. Roll 1 dough coil at a time into a 6-inch round with a rolling pin.

(recipe continues)

5. Preheat a nonstick 8-inch skillet over medium heat. Place 1 dough coil in the hot pan and cook until golden brown spots appear on the bottom, about 1 minute. Flip the paratha with a spatula and cook until golden brown spots appear on the other side, about 1 minute more. Drizzle 1 teaspoon of the remaining oil on the top side and press down with the spatula to cook. Flip and add 1 teaspoon oil to the other side and cook until golden and sizzling, about 1 minute per side. Repeat with the remaining coils of dough. Scrunch the parathas gently in your palms to break open the spiral layers. Store the cooked parathas in a container, loosely covered. Serve warm.

Sweet Potato Chip Chaat

SERVES 4

3 medium sweet potatoes (about 1 pound)

2 tablespoons olive oil

3 teaspoons chaat masala

1 teaspoon kosher salt

1 small Yukon Gold potato, boiled, peeled, and cut into ¼-inch cubes

3 tablespoons Cilantro Chutney (page 4)

3 tablespoons Date & Tamarind Chutney (page 62)

2 tablespoons plain plant-based yogurt

Garnishes

¼ cup finely diced red onion

¼ cup chopped fresh cilantro

¼ cup sev (optional; see Note)

2 tablespoons pomegranate seeds

Chaat is the gateway for falling in love with Indian food. I once described chaat as the cousin of nachos—they are not exactly similar, but the concept of a base, toppings, and sauces got across. I'll always double down for traditional fried chaat, but during summertime I lighten things up by roasting the sweet potatoes.

1. Preheat the oven to 425°F. Line a baking sheet with foil.

2. Peel the sweet potatoes and cut into rounds about ¼ inch thick. In a large bowl, toss the sweet potatoes with the olive oil, 2 teaspoons of the chaat masala, and the salt. Spread the sweet potatoes on the prepared baking sheet and bake for about 30 minutes, until tender, tossing them halfway through baking.

3. To assemble, pile the sweet potatoes on a serving dish with the cubed Yukon Gold potato on top. Dollop with the chutneys and yogurt. Sprinkle the remaining 1 teaspoon chaat masala over the top. Garnish with red onion, cilantro, sev (if using), and pomegranate seeds and serve.

NOTE: *Sev is a type of crispy noodle made from flour, water, and salt. Sev can be eaten plain or used as a topping for chaat dishes. Purchase ready-made sev at any Indian grocery store or online.*

Left: **Fire-Roasted Corn (page 176);** *right:*
Tandoori Mushroom Skewers (opposite)

Tandoori Mushroom Skewers

SERVES 2 TO 4

One 8-ounce container
cremini mushrooms

1 large red onion, cut into
large cubes

3 tablespoons Tandoori
Masala (page xxiv)

Kosher salt

3 tablespoons neutral oil

Lemon wedges, for serving

Mushrooms can take center stage on the grill—and there are
so many varieties to experiment with: lion's mane, shiitakes,
and oyster and also the ubiquitous trio of buttons, cremini, and
portobellos, which are widely available year-round. Mushrooms are
woodsy and smoky; marinated with tandoori masala and grilled,
they are a wonderful substitute for meat. These mushroom skewers
can be prepped the night before and grilled within minutes before
guests arrive. If using wooden skewers, soak them in water for
30 minutes before grilling.

1. Preheat a gas grill to 400°F.

2. Place the mushrooms in a microwave-safe bowl with ¼ cup water
and microwave for 2 minutes. Let cool for 10 minutes, then drain
the liquid.

3. Transfer the precooked mushrooms to a large bowl and add the
onion. Sprinkle with the tandoori masala and salt to taste. Add the
oil and toss to combine. Alternate the mushrooms and diced onion
on metal or soaked wooden skewers. Grill the mushrooms on the
hotter side of a hot two-level fire (cover the grill if using gas), flipping
every 2 minutes until the mushrooms and onion are charred on all
sides. Transfer the skewered vegetables to a serving plate and serve
immediately with lemon wedges.

4. For an alternative oven method, place an oven rack under the
broiler and preheat the oven to broil on high. Arrange the precooked
mushrooms and onion evenly in a large cast-iron skillet and heat over
medium-high heat on the stovetop for 5 minutes, or until the onions
have softened. Give the vegetables a toss, then place the pan under
the broiler for 2 minutes to char the vegetables. Transfer them to a
serving plate and serve immediately with lemon wedges.

Fire-Roasted Corn (Masala Bhutta)

SERVES 6

½ teaspoon ground cayenne
1 teaspoon kosher salt
6 ears corn, shucked
2 limes, halved

Prepare to have your summer corn game elevated to the next level, because if you haven't tried roasting your corn directly on the flame of your stove, you're missing out! As the kernels get charred, they burst with a sweet and smoky flavor that's simply out of this world. And if you think regular corn on the cob is good, wait until you try Indian corn on the cob. It's a beloved staple in many households and sold on street sides and at train stations across India.

1. Mix the cayenne and salt in a small bowl and set aside.

2. Turn a gas burner to medium-high. Working with one ear of corn at a time, use tongs to place the corn directly on the burner. Cook, turning the corn every minute or so to ensure even charring. You'll notice the kernels will start to turn golden brown and black in spots and the corn will begin to emit a smoky aroma. Each ear will take 4 to 6 minutes to char. (The kernels will pop loudly, so don't be startled!) Once the corn is evenly charred, use tongs to transfer to a serving plate.

3. Dip the lime halves in the salt and cayenne mixture and rub over all the ears of corn.

4. Allow the corn to cool for a few minutes before serving.

NOTES

• To char corn on an electric or induction stove, preheat a cast-iron or heavy-bottomed skillet over medium-high heat for 10 minutes, add the corn and 1 teaspoon neutral oil, and cook, stirring occasionally and letting the corn char on each side, about 5 minutes.

• Buy fresh, young corn with tight, hydrated green husks and golden-colored corn silk (not dark brown).

Pea & Pistachio Tikkis

One 16-ounce can chickpeas, rinsed and drained

1 cup cooked bulgur

½ cup frozen green peas, thawed

½ cup raw unsalted pistachios

¼ cup roughly chopped fresh parsley

¼ cup roughly chopped fresh dill

¼ cup ground flaxseed

2 tablespoons chia seeds

1 teaspoon ground cumin

1 teaspoon ground coriander

1 teaspoon ground cayenne

1 teaspoon kosher salt

Juice of 1 lemon (about 2 tablespoons)

4 to 6 tablespoons neutral oil

Dash & Chutney Hot Sauce (page 164), for serving

Tikkis are cute little patties made with potatoes and peas, for a dish called aloo tikkis. I created this tikki-inspired recipe in preparation for an ayahuasca ceremony at a retreat in Costa Rica. I spent a month preparing my body with a regimented diet of no alcohol, coffee, onion, garlic, or spicy food, the latter being the most challenging for me to give up.

1. Place the chickpeas, bulgur, green peas, pistachios, parsley, dill, flaxseed, chia seeds, cumin, coriander, cayenne, salt, and lemon juice in the bowl of a food processor and pulse until the mixture is well combined but not pureed. Scoop out 1 tablespoon of the mixture and form it into a little patty. If it breaks apart easily, add water, a tablespoon at a time, to the mixture. Form the mixture into about 20 small patties, each about 2 inches in diameter.

2. Line a rimmed baking sheet with paper towels. Heat 2 tablespoons of the oil in a large skillet over medium heat until it is shimmering. Working in batches, sauté the patties until golden brown, 6 to 8 minutes, turning once. Wipe out the pan between batches to remove any loose bits of patty and heat an additional 2 tablespoons of oil for each batch. Transfer each batch of cooked patties to the prepared baking sheet to drain. Serve warm with hot sauce.

Dal with Broccoli Crumble

SERVES 4 TO 6

2 tablespoons neutral oil

½ teaspoon cumin seeds

1 medium yellow onion, chopped

2 garlic cloves, minced

1-inch knob fresh ginger, grated (about 1 teaspoon)

2 teaspoons ground coriander

1 teaspoon ground turmeric

1 teaspoon ground cumin

¼ teaspoon ground cayenne

⅛ teaspoon asafoetida (hing)

1½ cups toor dal, rinsed and drained

One 14-ounce can full-fat coconut milk

Kosher salt

Juice of 1 lemon (about 2 tablespoons)

2 pounds broccoli (florets and stems), trimmed and peeled, roughly chopped

1 cup walnuts, almonds, or sunflower seeds

Lemon wedges, for serving

Dal is a staple in many cultures and households, and I'm amazed whenever I stumble on a version I'm not familiar with. The excitement of discovering a new recipe and putting my own spin on it is nothing short of thrilling. Indian dal is never pureed, but in the Middle East it's served as a creamy soup. Every bowl of dal is an opportunity for culinary adventure—here, I've included a few unconventional components, like my broccoli crumble to add a healthy green vegetable.

1. Heat the oil in a large Dutch oven over medium-high heat until it is shimmering. Add the cumin seeds and cook until they are sputtering, about 30 seconds. Stir in the onion, garlic, and ginger and sauté until translucent, 3 to 5 minutes. Stir in the coriander, turmeric, cumin, cayenne, and asafoetida and sauté until aromatic, about 30 seconds. Add 4 cups water, the dal, coconut milk, and ½ teaspoon salt. Increase the heat to high and bring the dal to a boil. Reduce the heat to medium-low, cover, and simmer, stirring occasionally, until the dal is tender, 25 to 30 minutes. Stir in the lemon juice. Taste and adjust the seasoning, adding more salt if needed.

2. Meanwhile, pulse the broccoli and walnuts in the bowl of a food chopper until the mixture becomes a fine crumble. Portion the broccoli into bowls and pour the hot dal over it. Serve immediately with lemon wedges.

NOTE: *Use your broccoli stems—they are just as tasty as the florets. Peel the tough outer skin with a peeler or a knife, then chop or grate to use in this and other recipes. Stem centers are sweet, crispy, and mild.*

Mushroom Keema Shepherd's Pie

SERVES 6

1 cup textured vegetable protein (TVP)

2 tablespoons neutral oil

One 1½-inch cinnamon stick

2 black cardamom pods

3 whole cloves

1 tablespoon cumin seeds

1 bay leaf

3 large yellow onions, chopped

4 garlic cloves, minced

2-inch knob fresh ginger, grated (about 1 tablespoon)

Kosher salt

2 tablespoons tomato paste

1 medium Roma (plum) tomato, diced

2 Thai chilies, chopped

2 tablespoons dried fenugreek leaves (kasoori methi)

1 teaspoon ground turmeric

½ teaspoon Kashmiri chili powder

½ tablespoon ground coriander

2 tablespoons soy sauce

12 ounces cremini or other white mushrooms

Juice of ½ lemon (about 1 tablespoon)

Freshly ground black pepper

1 cup frozen peas

2 tablespoons chopped fresh mint

Keema, made with minced meat (lamb, goat, or mutton) and cooked with onions, tomatoes, spices, and herbs, is popular in India and Pakistan. It's served as a curry, a stew, and as a filling for samosas and parathas. This plant-based shepherd's pie is my version. I replace traditional minced meat with a combination of textured vegetable protein (TVP) and meaty mushrooms. TVP is made from defatted soy flour, sold in dehydrated form, and can be rehydrated in water or broth. It has a chewy texture that is similar to ground meat.

Mashed Potato Topping

2 pounds russet potatoes

4 tablespoons plant-based butter, cut into small pieces

1 cup plain plant-based milk

Kosher salt and freshly ground black pepper

1. Place the TVP in a medium bowl with 4 cups hot water and set aside for 10 minutes to hydrate. Drain off the excess water and set the rehydrated TVP aside.

2. Heat the oil in a wide, heavy-bottomed ovenproof skillet over medium heat until it is shimmering. Add the cinnamon stick, black cardamom pods, cloves, cumin seeds, and bay leaf and cook for 1 minute. Stir in the onions, garlic, ginger, and 1 teaspoon salt and sauté until most of the onions are lightly browned, 8 to 10 minutes. Push the onions to the edges of the skillet, making a well in the middle. Add the tomato paste and cook, stirring, until the paste darkens in color, 2 to 3 minutes. Stir the diced tomato into the paste.

(recipe continues)

3. Add the Thai chilies, fenugreek leaves, turmeric, Kashmiri chili powder, coriander, and soy sauce and cook for another 2 to 3 minutes. Stir in the mushrooms and the rehydrated TVP and cook until the mushrooms have released their liquid, about 20 minutes. Stir in the lemon juice and season with black pepper to taste.

4. Place one oven rack in the middle position and another in the top position. Preheat the oven to 350°F.

5. Meanwhile, make the mashed potato topping: Wash, peel, and cut the potatoes into 1-inch cubes. Place the potatoes in a large pot and add enough cold water to cover by an inch. Bring to a boil over medium-high heat and cook for about 8 minutes. Pierce a piece of potato using a fork, if it inserts without resistance, the potatoes are ready. Drain the potatoes and return them to the pot. Reduce the heat to medium and cook for another minute or so to remove excess moisture. Toss the warm potatoes with the butter pieces. Pour in ⅔ cup of the plant-based milk. Whip the potatoes with an electric hand mixer on medium speed until smooth and creamy, adding the remaining milk, if needed, to achieve the desired consistency. Season with salt and pepper to taste.

6. Remove the skillet from the heat. Discard the cinnamon stick, black cardamom pods, and bay leaf. Stir in the peas and mint, then transfer the filling to a baking dish and top evenly with the mashed potatoes. Bake until the filling starts to bubble up, about 20 minutes.

7. Turn the broiler to high and place the skillet under the broiler until the potatoes develop a golden-brown crust, 2 to 4 minutes. Cool for about 10 minutes before serving.

Old-Fashioned, My Way

MAKES 2 COCKTAILS

2 sugar cubes, or 1 teaspoon cane sugar

2 to 4 dashes of Angostura bitters

4 ounces (½ cup) bourbon or rye whiskey

4 ounces (½ cup) Garam Masala Syrup (recipe follows on page 185)

Ice cubes

2 orange peels, for garnish

2 maraschino cherries, for garnish (optional)

I have a friend who took a master class on cocktail making. She's a renowned mixologist in New York with a decorated résumé, having managed an impressive list of bar programs. She told me once, "Everyone should have a good old-fashioned in their recipe arsenal." It seemed like good advice, so here's mine.

1. Place 1 sugar cube in the bottom of each of two old-fashioned glasses. Shake a dash or two of bitters directly onto each of the sugar cubes.

2. Muddle the sugar cube with the bitters using a muddler or the back of a spoon until the sugar has partially dissolved, creating a paste-like consistency.

3. Divide the bourbon, then the garam masala syrup, between the two glasses. Stir gently with a bar spoon to mix and allow the flavors to meld. Add a few ice cubes to each glass, filling it about three-quarters full. Continue stirring the cocktail for about 30 seconds to chill and slightly dilute the drink.

4. Rub the outer skin of the orange peels over both glasses, then garnish the glasses with the peels. If desired, drop in a maraschino cherry for an added touch of sweetness and visual appeal.

5. Serve immediately and enjoy indulging in timeless elegance.

NOTES

• The choice of bourbon or rye whiskey depends on your preference for a smoother or spicier flavor profile, respectively.

• Adjust the amount of sugar and bitters to suit your taste. Feel free to add a little more sugar if you prefer a sweeter cocktail or a few more dashes of bitters for a more pronounced bitterness.

Left: martini with cocktail onions;
right: Old-Fashioned, My Way (page 183)

Garam Masala Syrup

MAKES 2 CUPS

1 cup cane sugar

2 tablespoons Garam Masala
(page xxiii) or store-bought

Bring 1 cup water to a simmer in a small saucepan, remove it from the heat and add the sugar and garam masala. Stir until the sugar has dissolved, then let the spices steep for 10 minutes. Strain the syrup through a fine-mesh strainer into an airtight container and store in the refrigerator for up to 2 weeks.

Food Is
FESTIVE

What's your most treasured holiday or celebration?

Being festive is a wonderful way to infuse joy and positivity into our lives. It's about embracing the spirit of celebration, no matter what the occasion may be. Whether it's a holiday, a birthday, or simply a sunny day, being festive means taking the time to appreciate the good things in life and to share that appreciation with others. It's about creating an atmosphere of warmth and happiness through music, decorations, and food. Holidays and celebrations brim with emotions; their traditions and rituals connect us with our friends, our communities, and our shared history.

Diwali, as a kid and now as an adult, is the most festive holiday I celebrate. Growing up in India, I would see the front porch of our neighbor's house, where the diyas (oil lamps) lined up in ornate geometric patterns, and my eyes would sparkle. The diyas mirrored the kaleidoscope of colors all around me. In every corner of their home, oil lamps cast a warm, inviting glow, while strings of lights draped the walls. My parents' and relatives' laughter bubbled in a chorus of joyous voices that filled the air, while I occupied myself with a handful of vibrant rangoli colors on the porch. That childlike wonder is still present when I celebrate Diwali, a holiday that ignited the spirit of wonder and pure, unadulterated joy in me.

So whatever you're celebrating, pause to appreciate the significance of it and fully embrace the moment. These moments are a testament to the diversity of cultures and a reminder of the power of community, connection, and celebration.

Tangy Cashew Nuts

MAKES 2 CUPS

1½ tablespoons neutral oil

10 to 12 curry leaves

2 cups raw unsalted cashews

1 tablespoon amchur (mango powder)

1 teaspoon Kashmiri chili powder

¼ teaspoon Garam Masala (page xxiii) or store-bought

1 teaspoon kosher salt

After my beloved pistachios, cashews are my second favorite nut. During Indian holidays, dried fruits and nuts are revered as the ultimate offering when hosting, and when I was a child, cashews were considered a symbol of opulence—I remember feeling like royalty whenever I got my hands on some. This recipe combines sweetness from the cashews, a pop of tartness from the amchur, and some crunch from the curry leaves (which you can eat whole).

Heat the oil in a wide heavy-bottomed sauté pan over medium-low heat. Add the curry leaves and cook until fragrant, about 30 seconds. Reduce the heat to low, add the cashews, and sauté, stirring frequently, until lightly golden all over, 12 to 15 minutes. Sprinkle with the amchur, Kashmiri chili powder, garam masala, and salt and stir to mix. Remove from the heat and let cool before serving.

NOTE: *For crunchy cashews, make sure to cook them over low heat, otherwise they will be golden on the outside but still soft and raw on the inside.*

Green Apple Marmalade (Chundo)

MAKES 2 CUPS

3 cups grated Granny Smith apples (from about 4 medium apples)

1½ cups cane sugar

1 star anise

½ teaspoon kosher salt

⅛ teaspoon ground cayenne

⅛ teaspoon ground cloves

⅛ teaspoon ground cumin

NOTE: *Soft-ball stage, when cooking sugar syrups, occurs between 235°F and 245°F. You can determine whether soft-ball stage has been reached by dropping a spoonful of hot syrup into a bowl of very cold water. Dip your fingers into the water to gather the cooled syrup into a ball. If the syrup has reached this stage, it will easily form a ball while in the water but will flatten once removed.*

I remember watching my mom and aunts attend chundo-making classes during mango season, where they would spend hours making this condiment. If you were the kind of kid who used to eat ketchup straight out of the bottle, then you'll totally understand where I'm coming from with our love for chundo. This lesser-known Gujarati condiment is like a sweet marmalade. The traditional recipe calls for raw green mangoes, which are steeped in a sweet syrup with cumin, cayenne, and cinnamon. Raw green mangoes can be hard to come by, so I started experimenting with other fruits and found that green apples work best. Use as a sandwich condiment or as a pastry filling for a sweet and spicy twist.

1. Stir together the grated apples, sugar, star anise, and salt in a large saucepan until the sugar is moistened. Let the mixture sit until the apples release their juices, about 10 minutes.

2. Bring the apple mixture to a boil over medium-high heat, stirring occasionally. Reduce the heat to medium and simmer, stirring occasionally, until most of the liquid evaporates and the mixture is loosely glazed, 12 to 15 minutes. Use a candy thermometer to check the temperature; it should be between 235°F and 245°F for soft-ball stage. Another way to check whether the correct stage has been reached is to remove some liquid in a spoon, cool for a minute, then carefully pinch some between an index finger and thumb. When you separate your fingers, a thin string of syrup, up to 1 to 2 inches, should form. This indicates the right temperature has been reached.

3. Remove from the heat and stir in the cayenne, cloves, and cumin. Spoon the mixture into a glass jar that has a tight-fitting lid. Let it cool completely, uncovered, at room temperature, about 4 hours, then tighten the lid and store in the refrigerator for up to 1 month.

Chundo Apple Tart

1 frozen vegan puff pastry sheet, thawed

½ cup Green Apple Marmalade (Chundo) (page 191)

3 medium Granny Smith apples (about 1 pound), peeled, cored, and cut into ⅛-inch slices

2 tablespoons unsalted plant-based butter, cut into small pieces

1 tablespoon cane sugar

2 tablespoons pure maple syrup

My sister lives in France, and when I titled this recipe, we had a fun squabble about its name. With its rustic edges, this tart looks like what I would call a galette, but she sternly admonished me that it's more akin to a pomme tarte. Either way, it's a lovely appetizer, sure to impress your friends and family. Store-bought frozen vegan puff pastry is now widely available and useful to have on hand at any time of year, but it's a lifesaver during the busy holiday season. I always keep a package in the freezer to whip up this recipe. The puff pastry should be thawed—ideally in the refrigerator—according to the package instructions before using.

1. Preheat the oven to 350°F. Line a large baking sheet with parchment paper.

2. Roll out the puff pastry sheet into a 10 × 16-inch rectangle. Spread the chutney on the pastry, leaving a 1-inch border on all sides. Starting in one corner, arrange the apples lengthwise in parallel rows, overlapping them, on top of the chutney, then fold in the pastry border. Dot the apples with butter and sprinkle with sugar.

3. Bake for 20 to 25 minutes, until the pastry has puffed in the corners and is lightly browned and the apples have caramelized.

4. Brush the tart with maple syrup and cool on a wire rack for 15 minutes. Transfer to a cutting board. Cut in half lengthwise and then crosswise into individual portions and serve.

Sweet & Savory Granola

MAKES 5 CUPS

2 cups old-fashioned
   rolled oats

2 cups mixed raw nuts, such
   as walnuts, pecans, and
   pistachios

½ cup raw pumpkin seeds

¼ cup green or golden raisins
   or any other dried fruit

¼ cup coconut oil, melted, or
   neutral oil

½ cup pure maple syrup

1 tablespoon paprika

1½ teaspoons pink
   Himalayan salt

¼ teaspoon Kashmiri chili
   powder or ground cayenne

When it comes to granola, I've always found store brands to be a bit too sweet, so I set out to make my own version that's both sweet and savory and completely irresistible. I developed this recipe after hours of roasting granola and nuts to get the right balance. It's smoky and richly flavorful with a satisfying crunch in every bite. And the best part? It pairs well with cold beer and kept me energized when I climbed Mount Kilimanjaro—imagine what it will do for you.

1. Preheat the oven to 300°F.

2. Spread out the oats on a large baking sheet and toast in the oven for 10 to 12 minutes, until light golden brown. Transfer the oats to a large bowl, add the remaining ingredients, and mix well to combine. Wipe the baking sheet and line it with parchment paper.

3. Increase the oven temperature to 325°F. Spread out the granola mixture on the lined baking sheet in an even layer. Bake for 25 to 30 minutes, until the granola is lightly golden and crisp, stirring occasionally.

4. Remove from the oven and let cool completely. Transfer to an airtight container and store in a cool, dry place for up to 2 weeks.

Whole Roasted Cauliflower

SERVES 4

Coconut-Mustard Sauce

1 teaspoon neutral oil
1 large shallot, minced
1 teaspoon ground coriander
1 teaspoon ground cumin
½ teaspoon ground turmeric
One 5.4-ounce
  can unsweetened
  coconut cream
2 tablespoons spicy whole-
  grain mustard
Juice of ½ lime (about
  1 tablespoon)
Kosher salt

Cauliflower

Kosher salt
1 whole medium cauliflower
  head (about 2 pounds)
¼ cup olive oil
½ tablespoon ground
  turmeric
¼ teaspoon freshly ground
  black pepper
10 to 12 fresh curry leaves
¼ cup pomegranate seeds,
  for garnish

When entertaining, we all want to impress our family and friends. And what better way to do so than with a showstopping whole roasted cauliflower at the dinner table? As I transitioned to hosting more plant-based parties, I still wanted to create dishes that not only tasted great but also elicited those coveted oohs and aahs from my guests. This cruciferous vegetable is a blank canvas for creativity. Here, I blanch the whole cauliflower, outer leaves and all, in heavily salted water before roasting, which reduces the cooking time and also ensures the cauliflower is well-seasoned on the inside. It's then roasted with curry leaves and served with a tangy mustard sauce.

1. **Make the coconut-mustard sauce:** In a small saucepan, heat the oil over medium heat, add the shallot, and sauté until translucent, about 2 minutes. Add the coriander, cumin, and turmeric and cook for 30 seconds. Stir in the coconut cream, mustard, and lime juice. Season with salt to taste.

2. **Make the cauliflower:** Preheat the oven to 475°F.

3. Fill a large pot with water, heavily salt the water, and bring it to a boil. Carefully lower the cauliflower into the pot. Blanch for 5 minutes to partially cook the cauliflower. A sharp knife should have resistance when inserted. Drain and cool for 15 minutes, or until the cauliflower is dry to the touch.

4. In a small bowl, whisk together the olive oil, turmeric, 1 teaspoon salt, and the pepper.

5. Place the blanched cauliflower in a large Dutch oven or cast-iron skillet. Drizzle the olive oil mixture over the top and use your hands or a pastry brush to coat the cauliflower evenly. Top with the curry leaves

(recipe continues)

and roast the cauliflower for 25 to 30 minutes, until golden brown and a knife inserted into the center meets just a little resistance. Turn the oven to broil and char the top of the cauliflower, about 2 minutes. Watch it carefully so it doesn't burn.

6. Use a wide spatula to lift the cauliflower onto a serving platter. Using tongs, remove the curry leaves and reserve for garnish.

7. Spoon the coconut-mustard sauce on top of the cauliflower, then garnish with the curry leaves and pomegranate seeds. Cut the cauliflower into thick wedges and serve.

Chilled Peach Soup

SERVES 4

6 ripe peaches, or 4 cups frozen sliced peaches

¼ cup raw cashews

1 tablespoon olive oil, plus more for drizzling

1 small shallot, sliced

1 garlic clove, minced

1 teaspoon Dried Mint (page 17), plus more for garnish

1 teaspoon dried fenugreek leaves (kasoori methi)

1 tablespoon pure maple syrup

Juice of ½ lemon (about 1 tablespoon)

Kosher salt and freshly ground black pepper

NOTE: *If using frozen sliced peaches, bake from frozen at 375°F for about 35 minutes, until peaches are tender.*

Get ready for a flavor explosion that'll transport you straight to the sweet peach orchards of Georgia! This chilled soup is my love letter to the Peach State, where my family has lived for thirty years. As a bona fide southern belle, I know a thing or two about crafting dishes that pay homage to the South. But this recipe, which incorporates cashews, mint, and fenugreek, isn't your typical southern fare. My secret is first baking the peaches until they're perfectly caramelized and imbued with a rich, indulgent butterscotch flavor. What's more, you don't have to wait until peach season to whip this up. I've found that frozen peaches work just as well as fresh, delivering the same silky-smooth finish.

1. Preheat the oven to 375°F.

2. Halve the peaches and remove their pits, then place cut side up in a medium baking dish. Bake until the peaches are tender, about 30 minutes.

3. Place the cashews in a small bowl and cover with hot water. Set aside.

4. Heat the olive oil in a medium pot over medium heat and sauté the shallot and garlic until translucent, about 2 minutes. Stir in the baked peaches, dried mint, fenugreek leaves, maple syrup, and lemon juice. Cook until the peaches soften and their juices are released, about 10 minutes.

5. Place the peach mixture in a high-speed blender. Add the soaked cashews and 1 cup water and puree until velvety, about 2 minutes. Season to taste with salt and pepper. Chill for 4 hours. Garnish with a pinch of dried mint and a drizzle of olive oil and serve.

Shaved Brussels Sprouts

SERVES 4

1 pound Brussels sprouts, trimmed

2 navel oranges

2 tablespoons neutral oil

1 teaspoon black mustard seeds

¼ teaspoon ground turmeric

⅛ teaspoon asafoetida (hing)

Kosher salt and freshly ground black pepper

¼ cup toasted pumpkin seeds

1 tablespoon spicy mustard

I'll confess something: The traditional roasted Brussels sprouts I used to make for a Thanksgiving side dish were never a hit. They'd sit on the table, overlooked by my family, leaving me with a heap of leftovers that my mom and I would later repurpose by combining with black mustard seeds. To that mixture, I started adding juicy citrus segments and sparkling pomegranate seeds, and now this dish is a beloved staple on the Thanksgiving menu.

1. Using a mandoline or a sharp knife, shave the Brussels sprouts into thin slices and place them in a large bowl. Grate 2 teaspoons zest from the oranges over the top and set the oranges aside.

2. Heat the oil in a large sauté pan over medium-high heat until it is shimmering. Add the mustard seeds and cook until they sputter, about 1 minute. Add the turmeric, asafoetida, and shaved Brussels sprouts. Season to taste with salt and pepper. Sauté until the Brussels sprouts are tender but still bright green, about 3 minutes. Remove from the heat, stir in the pumpkin seeds and mustard, and set aside to cool.

3. To segment the oranges: Cut off the top and bottom of the oranges so they can stand upright. Using a sharp knife, cut away the skin and white pith from each orange, starting from the top and following the curve of the fruit. Once the skin and pith have been removed, hold the orange over a small bowl and carefully slice along the sides of each membrane, between each segment, to release the fruit. Be sure to slice as close to the membrane as possible to avoid wasting any of the fruit. Repeat until you have removed all the segments. Discard the membranes. Reserve any juice that has collected in the bowl.

4. Place the Brussels sprouts in a serving bowl and mix in the orange segments and the reserved juice. Serve warm or at room temperature.

Pea and Edamame Kachoris (Lilva Kachoris)

MAKES 40 KACHORIS

Filling

1 cup frozen peas, thawed

1 cup frozen edamame, thawed

2 tablespoons unsweetened shredded coconut, toasted

1-inch knob fresh ginger, grated (about 1 teaspoon)

2 tablespoons neutral oil

½ teaspoon ground cumin

½ teaspoon Garam Masala (page xxiii) or store-bought

½ teaspoon ground coriander

¼ teaspoon ground cayenne

¼ teaspoon ground turmeric

½ teaspoon cane sugar

⅛ teaspoon ground cinnamon

Kosher salt

Juice of ½ lime (about 1 tablespoon)

2 tablespoons finely chopped raw cashews

½ cup chopped fresh cilantro

Dough

2 cups all-purpose flour

1 teaspoon kosher salt

Neutral oil

Cilantro Chutney (page 4), Date & Tamarind Chutney (page 62), or plain plant-based yogurt, for serving

I love this Gujarati dish, filled with two types of peas, including the fresh and vibrant pigeon pea (lilva). To make it more accessible, I replaced the traditional lilva with edamame, which has a similar texture and is more readily available. Every time my family comes together to make this dish, it's a bonding experience that transcends mere food prep. The tightly run assembly line, with each person assigned a specific task of portioning the dough, rolling, stuffing, and frying, is a symphony of love and tradition. And while everyone has their designated roles, it's my brothers who have the fun job of eating the first batch of these bites of heaven.

1. Make the filling: Place the peas, edamame, coconut, and ginger in the bowl of a food chopper and pulse to a coarse paste.

2. Heat the oil in a 10-inch sauté pan over medium heat. Add the pea mixture and cook, stirring well, for 4 to 5 minutes.

3. Stir in the cumin, garam masala, coriander, cayenne, turmeric, sugar, and cinnamon and cook until there is no moisture left in the pan but the peas are still brightly colored, another 5 to 7 minutes. Season the mixture with salt to taste. Add the lime juice, cashews, and cilantro and mix well. Remove from the heat and transfer the pea mixture to a medium bowl to cool completely.

4. Make the dough: Place the flour in a large bowl and make a well in the center. Add the salt and 3 tablespoons oil to the well, then rub the mixture together using your fingertips and mix thoroughly to incorporate the salted oil with the flour. Add ½ cup cold water, a tablespoon at a time, and knead the dough until it is soft to the touch, adding more liquid as needed. Rest the dough, covered, for 30 minutes.

(recipe continues)

5. When ready to make the fritters, rub a little oil over the dough to create a smooth surface. Pinch off a small piece, approximately the size of a small apricot, and then roll it into a 3-inch round. (Alternatively, you can use a biscuit cutter to make an even round.)

(recipe continues)

6. Place about 1 tablespoon of filling in the center of the dough. Bring the edges of the dough up around the filling, pinching it tightly. Press the edges together at the top to seal. Trim off any excess dough with a knife. Roll the filled dough into a ball using the palms of your hands. Repeat with the remaining dough.

7. Fill a Dutch oven or heavy-bottomed pot with 3 inches of oil and heat it to 300°F. Working in batches, use a strainer to carefully lower the kachori into the hot oil. Fry until the pastry is golden brown, about 5 minutes. Place the cooked kachori onto a plate lined with a paper towel to drain before serving. Serve hot or at room temperature with chutney or yogurt alongside. Freeze any uncooked or cooked filling in an airtight container for up to 1 month.

Pav Bhaji

SERVES 4 TO 6

2 large Yukon Gold potatoes, peeled and cubed

1 tablespoon neutral oil

1 teaspoon cumin seeds

1 medium yellow onion, chopped

4 tablespoons plant-based butter

½-inch knob fresh ginger, chopped (about ½ teaspoon)

2 garlic cloves, chopped

1 Thai chili, chopped

2 tablespoons tomato paste

4 medium Roma (plum) tomatoes, diced

2 tablespoons Pav Bhaji Masala (page xxiii) or store-bought

1 tablespoon ground coriander

2 teaspoons Kashmiri chili powder

1 teaspoon ground cumin

1 teaspoon Garam Masala (page xxiii) or store-bought

½ teaspoon ground turmeric

1 tablespoon cane sugar

Kosher salt

One 16-ounce bag frozen California mixed vegetables

Half a 10-ounce bag frozen cauliflower rice, thawed

1 small green bell pepper, cored, seeded, and diced

Juice of ½ lemon (about 1 tablespoon)

Pav bhaji is the quintessential street food of Mumbai. The essence of Indian street food is so beautifully captured with this one dish—steamed veggies mashed with spices, smothered with a generous helping of butter, and cooked to perfection on a large griddle. This vegetable sloppy joe is a marvel. And here's a little secret—you can whip up a quick and easy version on a weeknight using frozen vegetables instead of chopping up fresh ones, which is what I do in this recipe. My sister has perfected this dish (sorry, Mom), and it's now a staple at all our family gatherings.

To serve

4 to 6 buttered burger buns

½ small red onion, chopped

½ cup chopped fresh cilantro

1 or 2 serrano chilies, thinly sliced (optional)

2 lemons, cut into wedges

1. Place the potatoes in a medium pot, cover with water, and bring to a boil. Cook over medium heat until soft, about 20 minutes. Drain and mash with a potato masher. Set aside.

2. Heat the oil in a large saucepan over medium-high heat until it is shimmering. Add the cumin seeds and cook until they sputter, about 30 seconds. Add the onion and butter. Sauté until the onion is translucent, 3 to 5 minutes. Add the ginger, garlic, Thai chili, and tomato paste and cook for another 1 to 2 minutes. Stir in the tomatoes and cook until they are soft, about 5 minutes. Add the pav bhaji masala, coriander, Kashmiri chili powder, cumin, garam masala, turmeric, sugar, and 1 teaspoon salt. Mix well and cook for 2 to 3 minutes, until fragrant.

(recipe continues)

3. Add the mashed potatoes, frozen vegetables, cauliflower rice, bell pepper, and ¼ cup water and mix well. Cook, covered, for another 15 to 20 minutes, stirring often, until oil beads on the surface. Using an immersion blender, potato masher, or the back of a ladle, mash the vegetable mixture into a mostly smooth puree (a little chunky is fine). Cook for about another 5 minutes, stirring occasionally and adding a splash of water if needed, until the mixture is homogeneous, slightly thickened, and the excess water has evaporated. Add the lemon juice and season with salt to taste. Mix well and cook for another 2 to 3 minutes.

4. Serve warm on buttered buns, topped with chopped onions, cilantro, and sliced serrano chilies (if using), with lemon wedges on the side.

Chocolate-Coconut Macaroons

MAKES 12 MACAROONS

½ cup coconut flour

¾ cup aquafaba (see page xxvii)

One 14-ounce bag unsweetened finely shredded coconut

One 7.4-ounce can sweetened condensed coconut milk

1 teaspoon pure vanilla extract

1 teaspoon ground cardamom

½ teaspoon kosher salt

⅔ cup vegan dark chocolate chips

Coconut mithai, a sweet dessert, is a ubiquitous sight at weddings, temples, and Hindu festivals. This delightful treat is about so much more than the taste—it's about the spirit of community, celebration, and love that it represents. Sharing little boxes of these sweets is symbolic and the essence of building and maintaining relationships. Traditional Indian mithai are a little too saccharine for my liking. That's why I came up with a lighter, less sugary version of this classic dessert in the form of macaroons.

1. Place an oven rack in the middle position and preheat the oven to 325°F. Line two baking sheets with silicone baking mats. (Alternatively, line them with parchment paper and spray with cooking spray.)

2. Toast the coconut flour in a medium skillet over medium-low heat until lightly golden, 3 to 5 minutes. Transfer to a large bowl to cool.

3. Once the coconut flour has cooled, pour in the aquafaba, then add the coconut, condensed coconut milk, vanilla, cardamom, and salt. Mix well to evenly moisten, breaking up any clumps with a rubber spatula. Chill the batter in the refrigerator for 15 minutes.

4. Using a small ice cream scoop or a spoon, drop the batter onto the prepared baking sheets, spacing the mounds about 1 inch apart.

5. Bake until light golden brown, 20 to 22 minutes.

6. Let the cookies cool on the baking sheets until set, about 20 minutes, then use a metal spatula to transfer them to a wire rack to cool completely.

(recipe continues)

7. Place the chocolate in a microwave-safe bowl and microwave for 30 seconds, then stir with a spatula, scraping down the sides of the bowl. Return the chocolate to the microwave for another 10 to 15 seconds, until it's almost melted.

8. Dip the bottoms of the macaroons into the melted chocolate. Return the cookies to the lined baking sheets and refrigerate for 7 to 10 minutes, until set. Store in an airtight container for up to 1 week.

Coconut Rice Pudding (Kheer) with Butterscotch

SERVES 4

Salted Vanilla Butterscotch

8 tablespoons (1 stick) unsalted plant-based butter, cut into small pieces

1 cup cane sugar

One 5.4-ounce can unsweetened coconut cream

1½ teaspoons kosher salt

1 teaspoon ground cardamom

¼ teaspoon ground cinnamon

¼ teaspoon ground cloves

Pinch of freshly grated nutmeg

Rice Pudding

2 cups barista-style plain oat milk

One 15-ounce can full-fat coconut milk

One 5.4-ounce can unsweetened coconut cream

One 1½-inch cinnamon stick

3 green cardamom pods

½ teaspoon ground cardamom

½ cup Arborio rice or other short-grain rice

¼ cup cane sugar

¼ teaspoon kosher salt

¼ cup large unsweetened coconut flakes

Picture this: You're at an Indian wedding, surrounded by a sea of colors, music, and laughter. Amid all this celebration, a humble dessert that's lavishly topped with saffron, nuts, dried fruit, and rose petals catches your eye—kheer, a traditional, comforting Indian rice pudding. Kheer is an embodiment of Indian culture, family values, and traditions, synonymous with celebration. This is one instance when you should *not* use basmati rice; short-grain rice will give this pudding its creamy texture. I use Arborio, an Italian rice used for risotto.

1. **Make the salted vanilla butterscotch:** Melt the butter in a medium saucepan over medium heat. Add the sugar, stirring occasionally with a wooden spoon, until the butter and sugar turn a medium amber color, 5 to 6 minutes. (Watch for the bubbles to reduce and the mixture to look glossy.) Remove from the heat.

2. Whisk together the coconut cream, salt, cardamom, cinnamon, cloves, and nutmeg. Put on oven mitts before carefully pouring a third of the coconut mixture into the caramel mixture—the caramel will spurt and bubble up. Once the caramel has settled down again, pour in the remaining coconut mixture and stir well to combine. Let the mixture cool to room temperature, about 30 minutes, then strain through a fine-mesh strainer into a medium bowl. (If not using right away, store the sauce in an airtight container in the refrigerator for up to 1 week. Reheat it gently over low heat before using.)

3. **Make the rice pudding:** Heat the oat milk, coconut milk, and coconut cream in a medium saucepan over medium-low heat until warm, about 4 minutes. Reduce the heat to low and stir in the cinnamon stick, cardamom pods, and ground cardamom. Add the rice

(recipe continues)

and cook, stirring frequently, scraping the bottom to prevent the rice from sticking, until the cream begins to thicken, about 20 minutes. Stir in the sugar and salt and continue to cook, stirring frequently, until the rice is cooked and the sugar has melted, about 10 more minutes. Remove from the heat, discard the cinnamon stick and cardamom pods, and set aside to cool slightly.

4. While the pudding is cooling, heat a 10-inch skillet over medium-low heat. Spread out the coconut flakes in a thin layer in the skillet and toast, stirring frequently, until the coconut smells nutty and is lightly golden. Remove from the heat.

5. Divide the pudding among four bowls. Drizzle with the butterscotch sauce, top with toasted coconut flakes, and serve.

Food Is
INDULGENT

What foods give you goose bumps?

Indulgent foods are the essence of bliss, generating at first bite an intense emotional and sensory interplay, slowing time and creating a symphony of pleasure.

For me, the simple act of cooking and eating indulgent foods is rife with moments of unabashed and undeniable pleasure. I savor the remnants from a mixing bowl, delight in the sensation of a warm cinnamon bun disintegrating on my tongue, or relish the fluffy clouds in my whipped coffee. My senses are automatically awakened by the memory of a chocolate-drenched truffle melting seductively on my tongue or the brief hypnotic pause of my brain at the aroma of freshly baked pastries.

Experiencing food in this immersive way is an unequivocal pursuit of pleasure, one that elevates the mere act of baking or eating into a truly divine encounter. Indulgent foods wield the transformative power to momentarily whisk us away from the humdrum of the everyday and propel us into an otherworldly experience.

To fully appreciate indulgent foods, surrender is a necessity. These experiences beckon us to embrace the memories, emotions, and pleasures that accompany them.

Pistachio Butter

MAKES 2 CUPS
4 cups raw pistachio nuts

3 tablespoons neutral oil

NOTE: *To extend the shelf life of nuts and prevent them from becoming rancid because of temperature fluctuations, store them in the refrigerator or freezer rather than in the pantry or kitchen cupboard.*

Pistachios ooze luxury to me, with their delicate light green color and sleek exterior. Whether I'm nibbling on a few as a snack or biting into a dessert, I feel a bit fancier eating these little gems. I've become fond of pistachio butter for an everyday breakfast spread and as a dessert base. Try adding a layer of this nut butter the next time you make avocado toast.

Place the pistachios in the bowl of a food processor and pulse four or five times to start the butter. Process on high speed, scraping down the sides of the bowl as needed, for 2 to 3 minutes. Drizzle the oil and process until a thick paste forms, about 2 minutes. Transfer the pistachio butter to an airtight container and store in the refrigerator for up to 3 weeks.

Pistachio Butter Toast

MAKES 4 TOASTS

½ cup Pistachio Butter (recipe above)

¼ cup plain oat milk or other plant-based milk

2 tablespoons pure maple syrup, plus more for drizzling

¼ teaspoon ground cardamom

1 teaspoon rose water

Pinch of pink Himalayan salt

Four ¼-inch slices crusted bread, toasted

Toppings

Sliced strawberries

Pomegranate seeds

Once you've tasted this divine, goddess-worthy spread, nut butter toast will never be the same again. I'm utterly obsessed with this healthy yet indulgent morning luxury on a plate. Whether you're pampering yourself with a lavish morning meal or impressing brunch guests, this spread will take your toast game to the next level.

1. In a medium bowl, whisk together the pistachio butter, oat milk, maple syrup, cardamom, rose water, and salt to make a spreadable paste. (Alternatively, you can mix the ingredients in a small smoothie blender.)

2. Slather the pistachio mixture on the toast and top with fruit. Drizzle with maple syrup and serve.

Chocolate-Pistachio Cups

MAKES 12 CUPS

2 cups Pistachio Butter (page 220)

½ cup powdered sugar

¼ teaspoon ground cardamom

16 ounces vegan dark chocolate chips, or bar, chopped

1 tablespoon coconut oil

1 tablespoon Maldon salt, for garnish

2 tablespoons pistachio shavings, for garnish

This fusion of pistachio butter cups and York peppermint patties will bring back memories of Halloween—but with a grown-up twist. They're a little slice of chocolatey, minty heaven!

1. Line a standard muffin tin with paper cupcake liners. Line a baking sheet with a silicone baking mat or parchment paper.

2. In a small food chopper, process the pistachio butter, powdered sugar, and cardamom until smooth and well combined. Transfer the pistachio mixture to the prepared baking sheet. Using a spoon or your hands, shape the pistachio mixture into an ⅛-inch-thick 12 × 12-inch square. Freeze for about 1 hour, until the paste hardens. With a 1½-inch cookie cutter, punch out 12 rounds of the hardened pistachio butter mixture. Place the rounds, still on the baking sheet, back in the freezer.

3. Place the chocolate in the top of a double boiler or in a heat-proof bowl set on top of a pot of simmering water and melt over medium-low heat, stirring occasionally. Stir in the coconut oil and remove from the heat.

4. Remove the pistachio butter rounds from the freezer. Using a tablespoon measure, ladle warm chocolate into the bottom of the prepared muffin cups and tap the tin gently on the counter. Working quickly, set a pistachio butter round in the center of each cupcake liner and pour 2 tablespoons of melted chocolate on top. Gently tap the tin again to remove any air bubbles. Sprinkle the tops with the Maldon salt and pistachio shavings. Refrigerate for an hour or two, until the chocolate is set. Store the cups in an airtight container in a cool, dry place for up to 2 weeks.

Date & Nut Energy Balls

MAKES 20 ENERGY BALLS

2 cups chopped pitted dates, soaked in hot water for 5 minutes

2 tablespoons coconut oil, plus more for oiling your hands

1 cup raw cashews

½ cup raw walnuts

½ cup raw pistachios

1 teaspoon grated orange zest

½ teaspoon rose water

1 teaspoon pink Himalayan salt

When I sat down to write this book, I never could have predicted the incredible journey it would take me on. One of the most memorable moments was attending a conference in the heart of the Middle East, where I was lucky enough to discover the magic of dates. From the sweet and succulent Medjool to the small, luscious Barhi and beyond, I was in date heaven! And when I returned home with a few pounds of fresh dates, my mom and I whipped up this recipe together by cooking down the dates into a sticky, candy-like paste. To complement the sweetness, we added a pop of orange zest and a sprinkle of pink Himalayan salt.

1. Place the dates in the bowl of a food chopper and process into a paste.

2. Heat the coconut oil in a large skillet over medium-low heat, add the date puree, and cook until the dates have softened. Add the nuts, orange zest, rose water, and salt and stir until well combined. Gently warm through for another 5 to 7 minutes. Remove from the heat and let cool slightly.

3. Oil your hands to keep the mixture from sticking, and portion into 1-inch balls. Serve warm or at room temperature. Store leftover energy balls in an airtight container in a cool, dry place for up to 2 weeks.

Chai Sticky Toffee Cakes

Cakes

Cooking spray

4 black or chai-flavored
tea bags

⅔ cup boiling water, plus
more for the baking pan

1½ teaspoons ground ginger

1 teaspoon ground cinnamon

1 teaspoon ground cardamom

Pinch of freshly grated
nutmeg

8 ounces Medjool dates,
pitted and chopped into
small pieces

1 teaspoon baking soda

2 tablespoons ground
flaxseed

¾ cup all-purpose flour,
sifted

1 teaspoon baking powder

¼ teaspoon kosher salt

½ cup light brown sugar

4 tablespoons plant-based
butter, melted

1 teaspoon pure vanilla
extract

Toffee Sauce

One 14-ounce can full-fat
coconut milk

½ cup light brown sugar

¼ teaspoon kosher salt

Warm desserts are nearly impossible for me to turn down. Get ready to be transported to the cozy warmth of holiday markets with these toffee cakes! Every bite takes me back to wandering through Christmas markets in Europe with my sister, sipping hot drinks and snacking on sweet treats. This recipe, paired with the spicy warmth of chai, is my riff on a classic English dessert.

1. **Make the cakes:** Place an oven rack in the middle position and preheat the oven to 350°F. Line a deep-sided baking or roasting pan with a clean kitchen towel. Coat six ramekins with cooking spray, place in the baking pan, and set aside.

2. Brew the tea in the boiling water, steep for 5 minutes, then strain into a medium bowl and whisk in the ginger, cinnamon, cardamom, and nutmeg. Add half of the dates and the baking soda. Set aside.

3. In a small bowl, mix the flaxseed with 6 tablespoons water. Set aside.

4. In a medium bowl, whisk together the flour, baking powder, and salt.

5. Place the remaining dates in the bowl of a food processor and pulse three to five times. Add the soaked date mixture and its liquid, the flaxseed mixture, the brown sugar, melted butter, and vanilla. Process until smooth, about 10 seconds.

6. Transfer the wet mixture to a large bowl and fold in the dry ingredients until all the flour is evenly mixed. Using an ice cream scoop, distribute the batter evenly among the ramekins, filling each just over halfway full.

7. Fill the baking pan with enough boiling water to come halfway up the sides of the ramekins, making sure not to splash water into them.

(recipe continues)

8. Cover the pan with aluminum foil, sealing the edges tight.

9. Bake for about 40 minutes, until the pudding cakes are puffed and small holes appear. Carefully remove the pan from the oven, uncover, and poke small holes on top of each cake with a skewer or paring knife. Remove the ramekins from the water bath after 10 minutes.

10. Meanwhile, make the toffee sauce: Combine the coconut milk, brown sugar, and salt in a medium saucepan and bring the mixture to a boil, whisking to melt the sugar. Reduce the heat to low and simmer for 20 to 25 minutes, stirring occasionally. The sauce will thicken slightly—it's ready when it begins to cling to the back of a spoon.

11. Divide half of the syrup evenly over the 6 cakes and wait 5 minutes for the cakes to absorb it. Spoon on the remaining syrup and serve. Cover tightly with plastic wrap and store in the refrigerator for up to 3 days.

Black Sesame Cinnamon Rolls

MAKES 9 LARGE ROLLS

Flour Paste

¼ cup bread flour

Filling

1¼ cups dark brown sugar

⅓ cup black sesame seeds, ground to a powder

2 tablespoons ground cinnamon

2 tablespoons plant-based butter, melted

Dough

⅔ cup plain oat milk or any plant-based milk

2¾ cups bread flour, plus more for the work surface

2¼ teaspoons (1 packet) instant yeast (see Note on page 230)

¼ cup cane sugar

1 teaspoon kosher salt

6 tablespoons plant-based butter, melted

Neutral oil, for greasing

Glaze

Two 8-ounce packages plant-based cream cheese, at room temperature

½ cup pure maple syrup

¼ cup plain oat milk or other plant-based milk

2 teaspoons pure vanilla extract

My mom and I made black sesame ladoos (round balls) at BAPS Hindu temple on Sundays. I have a soft spot for these cinnamon rolls with black sesame seeds that are reminiscent of those Sundays with my mom. When assembled, they create a bull's-eye pattern that's almost too pretty to eat. These rolls can be prepared the night before and baked early in the morning, filling the kitchen with an irresistible aroma of sweet cinnamon. Sinking your teeth into the warm rolls with gooey cream cheese oozing out all over your fingers feels so indulgent.

1. Make the flour paste: Whisk together the flour and ⅔ cup water in a glass measuring cup or other microwave-safe container and heat in the microwave for 60 seconds, stirring every 20 seconds, until the mixture reaches a smooth, pudding- or paste-like consistency.

2. Make the filling: Combine the brown sugar, ground sesame seeds, cinnamon, and melted butter in a medium bowl and mix until thoroughly combined. Set aside.

3. Make the dough: Transfer the warm flour paste to the bowl of a stand mixer fitted with the whisk attachment and whisk in the oat milk until combined.

4. Fit the stand mixer with the dough hook, then add the flour and yeast. Mix on low speed until all the flour is moistened, 1 to 2 minutes. Let stand for 15 minutes. Add the cane sugar and salt and mix on medium-low speed for 5 minutes. Stop the mixer and add the melted butter. Resume mixing on medium-low for 10 minutes longer, scraping down the dough hook and sides of the bowl when needed. The dough will be a little sticky.

(recipe continues)

NOTE: *If using active dry yeast, increase the amount to 2½ teaspoons, warm the oat milk for a few minutes (to 110°F), and bloom for 5 minutes before adding to the dough paste.*

5. Scoop the dough out onto a floured surface and knead the sides into the middle to form a round ball. Lightly oil a large bowl and the top of the dough to prevent a skin from forming. Place the dough in the bowl, cover with plastic wrap, and let rise until doubled in size, 1 to 2 hours.

6. Grease a 9 × 13-inch baking pan with oil.

7. Turn out the dough onto a lightly floured work surface. Gently press it to remove air pockets. Roll into an 11 × 8-inch rectangle with a long side facing you. Sprinkle the filling over the entire rectangle of dough, using your hands to spread it evenly. Press lightly to adhere the mixture to the dough.

8. Starting at the long edge near you, gently roll the dough into a loose cylinder (about 3 inches thick), taking care not to roll too tightly (if too tightly rolled, the rolls will rise upward).

9. Portion out 9 even pieces by marking the dough cylinder with a sharp knife, then cut the rolls along those marks.

10. Transfer the slices, swirl side down, to the prepared baking pan. Cover the pan tightly with plastic wrap and let the dough rise in a warm place until the buns are puffy and touching one another, about 1 hour. (You can also let them rise overnight in the refrigerator.)

11. Preheat the oven to 350°F.

12. **Make the glaze:** In a medium bowl, whisk together the cream cheese, maple syrup, oat milk, and vanilla until smooth.

13. Bake the rolls for 30 to 35 minutes, until golden brown. Spread half of the glaze on them while warm. Let cool for 20 minutes and then drizzle on the remaining glaze and serve.

Whipped Coffee

MAKES 4 CUPS

¼ cup instant coffee

¼ cup cane sugar

¼ teaspoon ground cinnamon, plus more for garnish

⅛ teaspoon ground cardamom

4 cups plain oat milk or any other plant-based milk, hot

¼ cup evaporated coconut milk (optional)

There's something wonderous about whipped coffee—it's a luxurious indulgence that you can enjoy without ever leaving your kitchen. While the TikTok crowd may have recently glamorized this trend, my aunt was way ahead of the curve back in the eighties. I can still hear her clanking a steel spoon against a mug, whipping up a frothy, delicious cup of coffee on demand. Although the process is simple, the results are showstopping—a stunning, velvety swirl that's as mesmerizing to look at as it is to drink. As someone who savors life's little pleasures, I can't get enough of these small moments of indulgence.

1. Place the coffee, sugar, cinnamon, and cardamom in a medium metal bowl, add 3 tablespoons hot tap water, and stir to combine. Use a large whisk or an electric hand mixer to whisk until the mixture is light in color and holds a firm peak, 3 to 4 minutes.

2. Divide the oat milk among four cups, and stir 1 heaping tablespoon of whipped coffee into each cup. If desired, for added indulgence, stir 1 tablespoon evaporated milk into each cup. Spoon any remaining coffee mixture on top. Garnish the top of each cup with a pinch of cinnamon and serve.

Acknowledgments

To all the women in my family who have come before me, who have broken down barriers and paved the way for me to be able to write this cookbook: I am honored to get to tell your stories. You have shown me the importance of family and food, and how they can bring people together. I am so proud to be the first female cookbook author in my entire family history. Thank you for your courage, your support, and your unconditional love. To my grandmothers, who have passed down their recipes and their stories to me: I cherish your memories and your traditions. To my mom, Nirmala, who taught me how to cook from a young age: I am so grateful for your love of food and for sharing that gift with me. It has allowed me to express myself creatively throughout my life. To my dad, Kirit, you are my inspiration and everything in life. To my sister, Jigna, for being my original editor, long before I had a book deal. Your love and praise mean the world to me. To my brothers, Durgesh and Krupesh, for challenging me to be better and for being my sous-chefs and my champions.

To my friends, who have supported me throughout this journey: I am so grateful for your constant encouragement. You always make me feel like I can do anything.

Nina, you've been my cheerleader for more than two decades, and I'm grateful to be celebrating this moment with you. Kamael, your consistent support is invaluable to my life. Susan, your love has taught me to believe in myself and to express my own love confidently. Mona, your sisterhood has been one of the greatest gifts I could ever ask for. Taryn, you've set the bar high, and I love following in your footsteps. Adam and Ana, I have no words for the love you've poured into our cookbook; it's evident in every photograph. Tracy, your friendship and effortless styling for photo shoots are something that I'll always cherish. Troy and Sandy, you are like my extended family, and I can't imagine my life without you both. Narda, your friendship and enthusiasm for my cooking make me smile.

To my agents, Sarah Passick and Mia Vitale: You believed in my project from the beginning, and you never gave up on me. You were always there to offer guidance and support, and you helped me to navigate the publishing process with ease. I am so grateful for your insights and expertise. You helped me to refine my vision for this cookbook.

To my editor, Sarah Pelz, and the entire team at Harvest: I am also grateful for your patience and understanding throughout the writing process. Thanks for making my work shine and for your careful eye on every detail of this book. Cynthia and Virginia, thank you for meticulously testing my recipes.

And finally, to my readers: Thank you for picking up this cookbook. I poured my heart and soul into it, and I hope that it sparks a deeper love for food and connection in you.

Thank you for being a part of my journey.

Universal Conversion Chart

Oven temperature equivalents

250°F = 120°C   325°F = 160°C   400°F = 200°C   475°F = 240°C

275°F = 135°C   350°F = 180°C   425°F = 220°C   500°F = 260°C

300°F = 150°C   375°F = 190°C   450°F = 230°C

Measurement equivalents

Measurements should always be level unless directed otherwise.

⅛ teaspoon = 0.5 mL

¼ teaspoon = 1 mL

½ teaspoon = 2 mL

1 teaspoon = 5 mL

1 tablespoon = 3 teaspoons = ½ fluid ounce = 15 mL

2 tablespoons = ⅛ cup = 1 fluid ounce = 30 mL

4 tablespoons = ¼ cup = 2 fluid ounces = 60 mL

5⅓ tablespoons = ⅓ cup = 3 fluid ounces = 80 mL

8 tablespoons = ½ cup = 4 fluid ounces = 120 mL

10⅔ tablespoons = ⅔ cup = 5 fluid ounces = 160 mL

12 tablespoons = ¾ cup = 6 fluid ounces = 180 mL

16 tablespoons = 1 cup = 8 fluid ounces = 240 mL

Index

About the Author

Palak Patel is a classically French-trained chef from the prestigious Institute of Culinary Education (formerly the French Culinary Institute), a TEDx speaker, restaurateur, and media personality.

She won the Food Network's famed *Chopped* and *Beat Bobby Flay* and was also a finalist on *Food Network Star* season 14. Most recently, Palak appeared as a guest judge on Food Network's competition series *Money Hungry* that aired in summer 2021. She also hosted a digital series with Food Network called *Diwali Menu*.

Palak has partnered with high-profile brands and made on-camera appearances on *Today*, *Good Day Atlanta*, and Food52 digital. Chef Patel was featured in an article entitled "The Women of the Restaurant Industry Speak Out About Their Pandemic Experience" in *Forbes*. She was also featured in HuffPost, *People*, *Women's Health*, Thrive Global, Mashable, Epicurious, *Bon Appétit*, the *Los Angeles Times*, and *India Abroad* and has made the cover of Atlanta's *Simply Buckhead* magazine as a rising star to watch in 2021 and beyond.

Palak moved to the United States when she was twelve. Her style of cooking is influenced by her childhood in India and time spent working in the South of France, San Francisco, and New York City. But she credits her mother, grandmothers, and aunts—the most influential women in her life—as her first culinary teachers.

HarperCollins books may be purchased for educational, business, or sales promotional use. For information, please email the Special Markets Department at SPsales@harpercollins.com.

FIRST EDITION

Designed by Melissa Lotfy

All photography by Adam Milliron except:
Pages x, xxii, xxvii, 233 by Shay Paresh
Page 246 by Kseniya Berson

Food styling by Ana Kelly

Leaf pattern © Leavector/Shutterstock; border on page iii © Katika/Shutterstock

Library of Congress Cataloging-in-Publication Data has been applied for.

ISBN 978-0-06-332064-2

24 25 26 27 28 IMG 10 9 8 7 6 5 4 3 2 1